On Opera

On Opera

Bernard Williams

YALE UNIVERSITY PRESS
NEW HAVEN AND LONDON

For information about this and other Yale University Press publications, please contact:
U.S. Office: sales.press@yale.edu   www.yalebooks.com
Europe Office: sales@yaleup.co.uk   www.yaleup.co.uk

Set in Minion by J&L Composition, Filey, North Yorkshire
Printed in the United Stated of America by Sheridan Books

Library of Congress Cataloging-in-Publication Data

Williams, Bernard Arthur Owen.
   On opera / Bernard Williams.
      p. cm.
   Includes bibliographical references and index.
   ISBN 978-0-300-08976-9 (alk. paper)
1. Opera. I. Title.
ML1700.W48 2006
782.1—dc22
                                                                        2006017015

A Catalogue record for this book is available from the British Library.

10 9 8 7 6 5 4 3

Contents

Editorial Preface

by Patricia Williams

My husband, Bernard Williams, was working on this collection when he was diagnosed with cancer. Acknowledging that time might be running out, he focussed on completing his final philosophical book (*Truth and Truthfulness*, published in 2002), hoping to turn back to writing about opera. Sadly, he died in 2003.

As as a teenager in the London suburbs, Bernard fell in love with opera. He collected records and went to performances of the Carl Rosa Company and Sadler's Wells, writing his own 'reviews' of operas and movies in a school exercise book. Many years later, to his great delight, he was appointed to the Board of the English National Opera (then Sadler's Wells) and later chaired the opera committee for three years when George (Lord) Harewood was managing director and after the company moved to its present home at the London Coliseum. Ideas for many of the essays in this book were conceived over the twenty years of Bernard's association with ENO during which time we saw almost every new production at ENO, Covent Garden and, later, at Glyndebourne.

George Harewood and his colleagues were devoted to the performance of opera in English so as to bring it to new audiences, to spotting and training talented young singers from Britain and the Commonwealth, and to the *esprit* of the company where rehearsals mattered and no-one flew in to be the star of the evening at the last minute. Artistically and musically, those were wonderful days. At the heart of it all was the brilliant and incredibly hard-working Charles Mackerras (musical director 1970–77) and the remarkable, and remarkably youthful, duo of Mark Elder (musical director from 1979) and David Pountney (director of productions from 1982). Through his pioneering and unforgettable performances, Mackerras had already introduced Bernard and many others to the operas of Janáček. A performance of *The Makropulos Case* at ENO prompted Bernard to reflect on the tedium of immortality: why the prospect of living forever made life itself meaningless and was therefore intolerable. The essay he later wrote became well known among philosophers but Bernard was more attached to it as a reminder of the inspirational power of Janáček's music.

I shall never forget the tremendous excitement and buzz in the foyer of ENO as bus-loads of people arrived from London and further afield (many of whom would never have gone to the Royal Opera House) to hear the *Ring* in English for the first time. The triumph of Reginald Goodall's *Ring*, completed in 1973, the special 'home-grown' achievement of Alberto Remedios, Rita Hunter, Norman Bailey and many other young singers and players made a whole new generation of Wagnerians of us all, including Bernard: 'On some evenings, when Reginald Goodall's patiently synoptic vision took hold, and Alberto Remedios showed what it is to be that very thing, a truly lyrical "Heldentenor", all the limitations disappeared, the creaking space-age scenery seemed to dissolve into light, and it was as if there were no tomorrow.'

Bernard gained a huge respect for the manifold skills that are vital to the creative, administrative and financial health of an opera house from observing the work and commitment of George Harewood himself, of Edmund Tracey, the wickedly funny and expert dramaturge, translator and supporter of singers, and Arnold (Lord) Goodman, the consummate negotiator and fixer. Extraordinary things were achieved, and in spite of all the familiar constraints of under-funding and financial uncertainty that opera in London faced, then as now.

Life as Provost of King's College, and the company of musical friends and colleagues in Cambridge also played a part in Bernard's thinking about opera. He was deeply proud and protective of the achievements of the Choir, and the role of the College in providing young musicians with a broad education in music and exposure to all a university had to offer before they began the formal rigours of professional training. He, rightly, took no credit for their success but he was delighted that former students and choristers – Robert Tear, John Eliot Gardiner, Andrew Davis, James Gilchrist, Judith Weir, Mark Padmore, George Benjamin, Gerald Finley, Matthew Best, Thomas Adès, Paul Daniel, Edward Gardner, Christopher Gillett and so many others – go on to make their names in the world of opera and music. Jonathan Miller's production, for Kent Opera, of *Così fan tutte* in Cambridge, prompted Bernard to think more about 'the problem' of Mozart's great opera. Opera was one of the many interests he and Jonathan shared and discussed over the years.

As a philosopher, Bernard was concerned with life and how it should be lived, with notions of truth and authenticity, with the role of luck in moral and political thought, with conflicting moral obligations in public and private life and with virtues and vices – in classical Greece, the Enlightenment, the Europe of Nietzsche and Wagner and the contemporary world. Such matters are at the very heart of opera as a dramatic art.

Barry Stroud, a fellow philosopher, has paid tribute to the grounded humanity of Bernard's philosophy:

> *He brought human life into philosophy, and so into the philosophy of all of us . . . The aspects of humanity he tried hardest to make sense of are among its most puzzling and difficult: the need to answer the question of how best to live, and then how to understand the possibility of so many different and equally defensible answers to the question. The challenge was always to make sense of humanity itself. Nothing transcendent, no principles of disembodied 'reason' or impersonal 'utility', will do. The answers can lie only within what is true of thinking and feeling human beings, their cultures and their histories and their aspirations.*
>
> *He brought human life into philosophy in another and more personal and so more immediate way. He exuded life itself in his own philosophising, as in everything else he did . . . You could not fail to be enlivened by his company and moved by the sheer enjoyment he felt for whatever engaged him. With Bernard, philosophy, for all its difficulty and seriousness, was filled with life, and it was fun.*

Iain Fenlon, a musicologist, also recalled what fun it was to share Bernard's passion for opera: 'Sheer delight, a sense of wonder at what music can do was immediately evident in Bernard's infectious reactions to performance.' He emphasised Bernard's fascination with 'the immediacy and the power of its [music's] emotional purchase, the ability of music to move both the heart and the intellect'.

But readers will find that it never was, or is, necessary to be well informed, or in the business either of music or philosophy, to enjoy these essays. When I first met Bernard he took me to a performance of *Tristan* at Covent Garden. So ignorant was I about opera then that it never occurred to me to wonder whether this choice of work or composer might be rather a test of our very new friendship. I never ceased to adore talking to Bernard about opera from that night on. Re-reading these essays is a vivid reminder of his gift for sharing his thoughts and his pleasures. I hope old friends and new readers will feel the same.

Editing the text

It is clear from his notes that Bernard had selected the essays for this volume and decided the rough order in which they should appear. He had intended to revise some of them and to add new material.

He would certainly have eliminated or reduced the overlaps and repetitions that are inevitable when essays written over a long period and for different purposes are read, end to end, as a continuous text. Michael Black and I have undertaken some of this work but decided it was preferable to accept a few remaining repetitions than to second guess what Bernard would have done. He might well have substituted alternative examples to illustrate some of the major arguments and themes which run through this collection. It is clear from his notes that one or two of the essays on Wagner, or on Wagner in combination with other composers, would have been merged into new and longer pieces.

Doubts were expressed about including the introductory article on 'The Nature of Opera' from *The Grove Dictionary of Opera* because, having been commissioned for a reference book, it is written in a different style from the rest of this collection. But Bernard had included it in his list of contents and several reviewers of the *Dictionary* found it a useful, if somewhat idiosyncratic, *tour d'horizon* for the general reader.

Bernard clearly intended to revise 'Rather Red than Black', the essay on Verdi, to take account of more recent scholarly work by Roger Parker and John Rosselli on the 'political' character of Verdi's early operas such as *Nabucco* and *I Lombardi*. But it was impossible to make out from his notes what he would have said. We hope the original (hitherto unpublished) essay will still give pleasure to a general audience without being seriously misleading.

Readers who are familiar with the published version of Bernard's commentary on *Opera and Ideas* by Paul Robinson (Chapter 12) will notice we have made cuts here to avoid excessive overlap with '*Tristan* and Time'.

We added the text of a more recent lecture (Chapter 15) to a gathering of musicologists because the ideas are of general interest to interpreters of music – conductors, singers, players and directors – as well as to their audiences. The aim is to outline the role of the musicological study of opera and the performance of opera; to distinguish between the different and distinctive conceptions of 'authenticity' which appropriately apply to music, to literary text and to music drama; and to touch on the complex problem of what might count as an artistic intention and what artistic aims at a given time for a given composer were even possible:

> *We have seen in the opera house in recent years the co-existence of two kinds of radicalism: an increasing 'authenticity' of orchestral and vocal performance, based on historical research, and productions and sets that display all degrees of rethinking and creativity up to the now notorious extremes of directorial whimsy ... What is significant in this is that two kinds of radicalism can combine to the same end – an uncluttered seemingly transparent enactment of what this particular work is.*

Although addressed to an academic audience, it is a good example of how philosophical skill can help to clarify notoriously confusing problems in a subject of general interest to music lovers.

I am very grateful to Michael Tanner for writing an introduction to the collection. I hope readers who look forward to Michael's opera reviews in the *Spectator* will be tempted by his recommendation to enjoy and argue with Bernard, as he himself did for so many years.

Keith Thomas put me on the spot, and spurred me on, when, at the memorial for Bernard at All Souls College, he expressed the hope that this volume would be published. Alexander Goehr was extremely encouraging when I had almost lost heart. Alison Latham's extensive editorial experience was very helpful. Iain Fenlon took enormous care in advising Yale University Press and helped to define what this book is about.

Robert Baldock's continuing enthusiasm and confidence in this project has meant a lot to me, and I am grateful for the care he and his colleagues at Yale University Press have devoted to it.

My greatest debt is to Michael Black – a staunch friend to us both from our earliest days. The combination of his editorial skill, judgement and musical knowledge has been essential to the enterprise.

Introduction

by Michael Tanner

Bernard Williams was a lifelong opera lover. He wrote often about operas, as well as being on the Board of the Sadler's Wells Opera before and after it became the English National Opera and moved to the Coliseum. Many of the pieces he wrote about specific operas were commissioned for programmes at ENO or the Royal Opera House at Covent Garden, others were given as talks on BBC Radio 3, in the intervals of opera broadcasts.

But Bernard was also concerned with larger reflections about the different ways in which the great opera composers achieve their dramatic ends, and was increasingly absorbed by 'the case of Wagner', as the most ambitious pieces in this collection show. Like all serious opera lovers, he was also deeply interested in music generally, and in drama apart from opera. (He wrote wonderfully about the Greek dramatists.)

One of the things that makes this collection of essays so impressive is that at no point does one get the impression, so familiar when philosophers write about the arts, that the 'message' of an opera is the thing that counts, as distinct from the 'medium'. Bernard, though one of the leading Anglo-American philosophers of his generation, was very well aware of the limitations of the discipline he professed: one of his most celebrated and discussed books is called *Ethics and the Limits of Philosophy*. It so happens that in the last couple of decades a surprising number of Anglo-American philosophers have shown an interest in opera – Peter Kivy, for example, Roger Scruton on *Tristan*, and Robert Schacht and Philip Kitcher on the *Ring*. But none of these has written so widely or, in my view, so illuminatingly as Williams, partly because he had no philosophical or cultural-political agenda to pursue. He was peculiarly aware of the individuality of each of the great composers of opera, and his essays always show a concern to be true to that.

Bernard's earliest passions were for Mozart and Verdi, and he was fortunate to be just old enough to go to Covent Garden for the visits of the Vienna State Opera in 1947 and La Scala, Milan, in 1950, so he was able to see and hear some of the great operatic artists of the time, both singers and conductors, without undertaking the then hazardous journeys to mainland Europe. These experiences, as well as performances by some of the leading singers in Covent Garden's regular company and its guests, gave him an appetite for great singing. He was present at Richard Tauber's last stage appearance, as Don Ottavio with the Vienna State Opera, and at Kirsten Flagstad's Isolde in 1948.

For Bernard opera was much more closely associated with particular performances than one might expect from a philosopher meditating on works, composers and the operatic form as a whole. He was acutely aware of the dangers, especially for anyone of an intellectual turn of mind, of abstracting from his actual experiences of opera in order to give a tidy but in fact inaccurate account of what the opera had been like as an experience, in the theatre or, less often, listened to on record. He loved to go to performances with people who were as passionately involved with operas as he was, and to argue with them afterwards, not so much about the performance as about what it had been a performance of. Many of my own discussions with him took place as he drove us back to Cambridge from London after performances by the ENO in the Coliseum. We had a broadly similar approach to opera, though he was suspicious of my unswerving attachment to the critical views of my 'master' F. R. Leavis, which I applied to opera just as much as to literature, and also of the extreme degree of my devotion to Wagner.

There was in Bernard, as anyone who knew him well would agree, a curious mixture of passion and detachment; not that the mixture is unusual, only its particular combination in Bernard's case. Moving moments and dramatic climaxes in opera, perhaps more than in the other arts, evoked a passionate response, and of a liberatingly immediate kind. I think one of the things he loved about Verdi's operas was the uninhibitedness with which his characters pour forth their feelings; certainly he enjoyed the vigour with which they hurl themselves into catastrophe, and the way in which they take any feeling that they have absolutely at its face value. In this he was at one with his close friend Isaiah Berlin, who wrote a celebrated and much-reprinted essay on 'The Naïveté of Verdi', which Bernard discusses in his essay called 'Naïve and Sentimental Opera Lovers'. In the course of that essay, as he moves towards his central concern, his differences with Berlin about Wagner, he doesn't express any doubts about what exactly Verdi's naïveté comes to, though he must have felt as unclear as I do about what that may be. When it came to Rossini, by contrast, I think Bernard was repelled by exactly what attracted the old misanthropist Schopenhauer (and the far from misanthropic Berlin): Rossini's depiction of people as puppets, jerked around by a force over which they have no control. That, at any rate, was how Bernard regarded the most celebrated Rossini comedies. He was very severe with any artist (not to mention any philosopher) who denied to human beings their full humanity, as he saw and felt it, and I think this was at the root of his devotion to Verdi and his coolness about the less great figures in the bel canto tradition that preceded him.

It is close to being a paradox about Verdi that although his subjects are usually gloomy, and the outcomes of his operas misery and death, and although that reflects Verdi's own view of the nature of the world, there is often, even usually, an enormous bracing élan to his music. It is fair to conjecture that a musical person listening to a Verdi opera without knowing the text or the drama would conclude that some lively enjoyment was being had by the persons on stage. That primal energy both appealed to Bernard and prevented him from feeling altogether as seriously about Verdi as he did about Mozart or eventually about Wagner.

There is something in this area which is worth thinking about. There are differing pleasures or satisfactions to be derived from opera, and the most enjoyable operas are not necessarily the greatest – a remark which Bernard confirms in quoting Berlin's remark that *Rigoletto* is the most enjoyable of operas. It offers in superabundance pleasures that are specifically operatic. And therefore, Bernard sometimes suggests, suspect. We might take the last act of *Rigoletto*. The events it depicts are appalling. In a seedy country inn a professional assassin gets ready to murder the licentious Duke, whose jester Rigoletto wants to have him eliminated since he has seduced Gilda, Rigoletto's daughter. Gilda turns up in disguise and offers herself instead of the Duke, and the assassin kills her and gives the body in a sack to Rigoletto, who gloats over the death until he hears the Duke singing, realises he has been tricked, opens the sack and finds his dying daughter within. Yet the drama is propelled by music consisting of, among other things, the Duke's singing 'La donna è mobile', the quartet, followed by the even more exciting trio, followed by the storm, then Rigoletto's discovery of his dying daughter, and their duet before she expires. Pure pleasure. Just as much as many other writers on opera during its four centuries, Bernard was preoccupied with the ways in which music can reinforce drama, or undermine it, or give it a kind of fascination which by any serious standards it shouldn't possess.

It was this last category of opera which Bernard wrote about in his pieces on *Tosca* and in his other remarks on Puccini. Like any musical person, he wasn't able to deny Puccini's extraordinary power, but he felt thoroughly suspicious of it, and was concerned to examine the mechanisms by which Puccini lures us into complicity with his own 'Neronic instincts', and those of his villains – though Bernard took *Tosca* to be the archetypical Puccini opera. His view is that Puccini takes devices that are common in opera and applies them with exceptional cunning, trading on our awareness of what those devices are and our enjoyment of the skill with which they are being deployed. My own feeling is that Puccini's effect on us is more visceral than that, and that Bernard's account won't apply to, say, *La Bohème*, which is just as potent, and which Bernard came to find as irresistible as even Stravinsky did. But the idea of Puccini as a singularly 'knowing' artist, who calculated his effects in a way and to a degree that few have managed, certainly is given a subtle and plausible account in Bernard's essay on *Tosca*, as is the idea that he is peculiarly manipulative, which one may well be inclined to agree with – I suspect most opera lovers are – while finding it difficult to explain how any artist who is careful about what he is doing is *not* manipulative. What makes Puccini perhaps unique in the history of the arts is the combination of a breathtakingly sophisticated technique, above all in the art of orchestration and in his handling of harmonic tensions over a vast period, with a genius for melody of a certain kind, and a tawdry vision of the world, or anyway an attachment to the box office appeal of presenting such a vision. Yet all opera lovers should ask themselves, as Bernard repeatedly did, whether the art form to which they are so attached is inherently prone to that kind of corruption. That is the kind of question to which one hardly expects an answer, but musing on it produces many invaluable insights, as we find in these essays.

Bernard occasionally laments how very small the amount of helpful operatic criticism is, and the situation in that respect shows no signs of improving. One the one hand we have opera lovers who are primarily interested in how well a particular favourite work of theirs is being sung and staged, with no concern for the value of the whole enterprise; and reviewers who merely do reports on the latest stagings and musical performances with no more general considerations in mind – they can be expected to have seen more productions of any given work than the majority of opera-goers, but they are no more serious. On the other hand we find academics writing essays or books which employ the latest literary-critical jargon, or more often that of the latest 'school' but one, and spin out their theories while vouchsafing no insights into the works they discuss, and so rightly have no impact on the interests of opera-goers. The questions, which it was routinely assumed that critics should deal with, of the meaning and significance of a given work of art, and also of the art form to which it belongs, simply don't get dealt with in most of what passes for operatic criticism.

They emphatically do in the essays in this collection, and in a spirit which links them to Joseph Kerman's seminal book *Opera as Drama*, which Bernard regarded with great respect, and refers to several times in his essays on Mozart and occasionally elsewhere. He had his suspicions about Kerman – about the extent to which he aspired to be the Leavis of opera, producing a constricted and 'puritanical' canon of works. Yet in the end Kerman's and Bernard's positions are close, with most of the same figures featuring in their operatic canons (though it's never clear whether that was what Kerman intended it to be), and for the same kind of reasons. Kerman was and is, of course, a distinguished musicologist, and the chapters in *Opera as Drama* are largely devoted to showing what are the specific and different ways in which the great composers made their musical contributions to the dramas in which their greatness is manifest. Bernard respected this, without feeling competent to do it. He also shared Kerman's tastes, with both Puccini and Richard Strauss being thought highly questionable, and *opera seria*, especially in its Handelian form, taken to be beyond resuscitation. Probably the enlargement of the operatic repertoire, not by newly written works, but by the incorporation of works then considered marginal, is the biggest single change in taste since Kerman and Bernard wrote. Bernard strongly admired the Glyndebourne production of Handel's *Theodora* in 1996, but that was an inspired staging of an oratorio. And certain composers who didn't get a mention in Kerman, or only a passing and slighting one, engaged Bernard, as we see in his essays on Janáček and Tippett, and in his occasional remarks on Britten, by whose operatic *oeuvre* he was fascinated, though he never had occasion to write about it.

Kerman was not, or claimed not to be, concerned with the human truth of the operas he dealt with. Bernard was extremely and explicitly concerned with exactly that, and hence his criticism is in the humanist tradition of literary criticism, as we find it in Samuel Johnson, or Arnold, or Leavis. His central operatic passion, for the Da Ponte operas of Mozart, is the most powerful evidence for this.

Bernard was writing at just the time that Mozart's mature operas were moving into the absolutely central place in the canon, and above all the period at which *Così fan tutte* was edging into a position which, only a few decades before, would have been unimaginable for it. I think no-one before Bernard had stressed the pain in *Così*, or at any rate had built that pain into a coherent and entirely favourable account of the work. Kerman thought that the opera got out of hand in Act II, with Mozart intent on giving the sisters' feelings, in particular Fiordiligi's, a seriousness which Da Ponte's libretto won't tolerate, so that a fissure arises in the opera, frivolity in the action gaping across at near-tragedy in the music. Bernard's answer to this in his essay on the opera is, if not definitive, at least profoundly illuminating. It seems still, to me, to leave unanswered the issue of how it is that Don Alfonso comes across as so loathsome a piece of work, for all, or all the more for, his geniality, while the action of the opera completely vindicates him. Perhaps that fact merely adds another dimension to a work which already leaves one disoriented.

If Mozart elicited from Bernard his most ardent criticism – I think that the classical balance, combined with the elegant intensity of Mozart, were his ideal – it was Wagner with whom in his later years he became ever more preoccupied. He had always listened to Wagner a good deal, and indeed was deeply involved in the inception and completion of the *Ring* in English under Reginald Goodall, which was such a milestone in operatic life in England, a unique and astonishing native achievement. But I think that the TV relay of the Chéreau-Boulez *Ring* in 1981–2 may have made Bernard both more critical and more enthusiastic about it, and about Wagner's work in general, than he had been, though, as he recognises, *Tristan* stands apart from the other music dramas, and Bernard's feelings about it were the most unequivocally favourable he had about Wagner. Of course, for many people *Tristan* is the Wagnerian work *par excellence*, and that is right in that it has some of Wagner's most characteristic features, above all a high level of erotic-emotional charge, from start to finish. It's also the work which casts the strongest spell over its hearers, and can lead them to wonder whether they are in safe hands. But just as Nietzsche and Thomas Mann, the two pre-eminent critics of Wagner, voiced doubts about his *oeuvre* but were unable to distance themselves from the miracle of perfection that is *Tristan*, so, apart from some doubts about King Mark, Bernard was lost in admiration.

In his most recent essay, 'Wagner and the Transcendence of Politics', which draws on other pieces he wrote over the years, it is the relationship between Wagner's artistic achievement and his expressed views on issues social, cultural, political and much else which gives Bernard pause. One extremely valuable feature of it is Bernard's dismissal of the superficialities of contemporary critics and some directors who rejoice in playing 'Spot the Jew' in Wagner's mature dramas, going through them and deciding that Mime and Beckmesser definitely are Jewish stereotypes, Klingsor is more of a marginal case, and so on. He points out that such readings are unable to influence one's response to these works in any serious way, and that the worrying thing about Wagner is not such correspondences, if they exist, but the way in which his personal beliefs can be felt to enter the very fabric of his works. It's not Mime's being in many respects a Jewish stereotype that matters, but the nature of Siegfried's heroism, or in Bernard's view the catastrophic failure on Wagner's part to realise that he hadn't created a hero in Siegfried, even if he wrote a funeral march of unexampled splendour when Siegfried is slain.

The subtlety of this critique of Wagner is enough to put virtually all combatants in the recent Wagner wars to shame. Bernard recognised the extraordinary potency of Wagner's art, and in part responded positively to it. But he couldn't and would not have wanted to respond with the single-minded ardour which so often characterises Wagner lovers, and which he thought of as a kind of mistake, an unawareness of the healthy qualities which Mozart and, in a completely different way, Verdi have and which Wagner wilfully lacks.

Like all Bernard's work, these essays are an invitation to argue. In their concision and the rigour with which he expresses himself they are a superb challenge to a sustained level of concentration on particular operas, and on the whole phenomenon of opera, which is, as I have said, even rarer than one might expect. They also convey his exhilaration at the sheer energy which attending an opera, or listening to a recording of one, can unleash in a person as responsive as he was, and as remarkably capable as he also was of articulating his responses with such rare conviction and intensity.

1

The Nature of Opera

Entry for The New Grove Dictionary of Opera

Definitions and borderlines

Opera is by definition staged sung drama, but that leaves many questions unresolved, some simply verbal, but others interesting for the nature of the form. 'Staged' represents a significant requirement. Operas can of course be given concert performances, and these are sometimes 'semi-staged', under conventions that allow some token costume, décor and movement. But works not intended at all for costumed theatrical presentation do not count. Sunk in financial disaster from his efforts with Italian opera in London, Handel turned to the oratorio, and the resulting works are not seen as a form of opera, simply because they were not designed for a theatrical style of presentation (though they do contain a number of what might be called stage directions). However, this example itself shows that, from a musical or stylistic point of view, less may turn on these classifications than one might assume. It has often been remarked that Handel's English oratorios can be intensely dramatic in their effect – sometimes more so than the examples of *opera seria* to which he had devoted his efforts in the theatre.

The main stylistic point that underlies the distinction between opera and oratorio tends to be the role of the chorus, which in oratorio is a constant presence and a major structural feature. But there are operas that deliberately reach for this effect (a recent example is Goehr's *Behold the Sun* [*Die Wiedertäufer*]), and there are other works that are sometimes presented in theatrical form and sometimes not, the most famous perhaps being Stravinsky's *Oedipus rex*, which, having been first performed, in 1927, as an oratorio and in the following year produced as an opera, has subsequently moved in and out of the theatre. In this particular case, the ambiguity marked by this history is central to the work, which by a variety of devices, including a Latin text, aims at a monumental neo-classical effect.

The requirement that opera be sung is unbreakable, though there are styles that question the distinction between speech and song, in particular the device of *Sprechgesang* developed by Schoenberg and his pupils. A more wide-ranging question concerns the amount or proportion of song that an opera should contain. *Recitativo secco* is unequivocally a form of song; controversy about its use, as contrasted with opera that is *durchkomponiert* (through-composed), has played an important part in the history of changing conceptions of opera, but the conventions of recitative do not call in question the identity of opera as song. The role of spoken dialogue, on the other hand, raises issues of genre that connect in curiously complex ways with matters of nationality, content, audience and performance style.

No-one denies that the German tradition of *Singspiel* has produced not only operas, but at least two of the greatest operas there are, *The Magic Flute* and *Fidelio*. A descendant of this tradition, also German-speaking but more associated with Vienna, is segregated under the separate name of 'operetta', presumably a diminutive of contempt for works that have a stereotypically frivolous plot and are often musically very thin. However, pieces in this style have regularly been performed by some leading opera singers, and there are at least two outstanding examples, *Die Fledermaus* and *The Merry Widow*, that have established themselves in the international repertoire of opera houses. In Vienna itself, there were two different houses, and the convention was that operetta did not appear at the Staatsoper; in Paris there were similar distinctions, between the Opéra at the Palais Garnier, the Opéra-Comique at the Salle Favart, and the Bouffes-Parisien, though the relation between the content of a given piece and the house in which it was produced was not altogether straightforward. In the French tradition, it was not the presence of spoken dialogue that made the difference between opera and operetta, any more than it did in the German case: what is perhaps the greatest of French operas, *Carmen*, has spoken dialogue in its original version. It seems a question rather of musical ambition and dramatic content. Not much French operetta has made its way into the international repertoire; the one work of Offenbach's to hold a steady place there is *The Tales of Hoffmann*, and that was called by him an opera (and produced at the Opéra-Comique).

With works originally written in English, the situation is different. For various reasons, virtually no work with English spoken dialogue is regularly produced in an opera house. The stage works with dialogue for which Purcell wrote music, such as *King Arthur*, are classed as plays, which moreover are dramatically unrewarding and demand discouragingly elaborate staging. In the eighteenth century, many ballad operas with dialogue appeared, and the most famous of them, *The Beggar's Opera*, is occasionally revived, but that effectively had no composer (the ballads were arranged by Pepusch), and indeed exists only as melodic line and bass. The works of Gilbert and Sullivan, the English parallel to Offenbach, have borne a peculiar relation to the operatic tradition, in part because of the historical accident that for decades a monopoly was exercised over them by the D'Oyly Carte Company, who imposed not only a stereotyped manner of production but also, and more significantly, a particular style of singing. Many of the performers were G & S specialists, who did not appear in the operatic repertoire. Now that the copyright has lapsed, some of the pieces have been successfully staged by an operatic company.

The most significant fact, however, about the English-speaking tradition is not the absence of partly spoken works which might be operas, but the immense success of a type of work with dialogue which is quite clearly not an opera, the musical. In English-speaking countries, it is the musical that has played the role in popular taste which, earlier, was played in Vienna by operetta and in Italy by Italian opera itself. To deny that the musical is opera is not simply a stipulation. It originated from operetta, in particular from the emigration of German composers to the United States, but it has developed in such a way that, at least as things now stand, the styles of dramatic performance and singing appropriate to it are different from those needed for most kinds of opera. The point has been sharply illustrated by opera companies' occasional attempts to perform musicals (*Kiss Me Kate* is an example), which are almost always unsuccessful, and also by the unsatisfactory casting of operatic artists in a recording of Bernstein's *West Side Story*, a work which tries to stand on the boundary between the two traditions.

In the 1980s there were signs of some convergence between a broadening taste for opera (associated with the immense success in various media of certain singers, notably Luciano Pavarotti) and popular musical theatre. However, this has not yet been translated into any worthwhile new forms. Several shows have tried to combine the form and appeal of the musical, compositional tricks taken from Puccini, and theatrical effects on a Meyerbeerian scale, and financially have been very successful, but in terms of anything except spectacle they fall below their sources.

The relations between opera and the other forms which are contrasted with it are thus complex, and the distinctions (in particular, that between opera and operetta) are to some degree arbitrary. The present position is that 'opera' is to some extent an evaluative term, used to refer to sung drama which is either 'serious' enough, or traditional enough in form and technique, to be staged in an opera house. (These criteria can of course themselves diverge: some bel canto works which are canonical examples of opera have virtually no serious dramatic content.) Moreover, history has had different effects on various national traditions. After Wagner's achievement, and the failure of his unnecessary attempt to distinguish his works from opera by calling them 'music dramas', it has come about that new operas almost inevitably have pretensions to being serious and often difficult works of art. The Italian tradition was most resistant to this modernist development, but its capacity to produce highly popular new works in what was indisputably an operatic tradition did not survive the death of Puccini. (It is tempting to speculate that the reasons why he was unable to write the love duet at the end of *Turandot*, his last work, were not just depth-psychological, as Mosco Carner well argued, but cultural: the Princess of Death, with her orchestral complexities, had claimed the popular tradition as well as her previous suitors.)

The entrenched division between opera as art work and other kinds of musical theatre, such as the musical, is presently expressed in differences of vocal and performance style. However, this in itself should not be insuperable: what is by general agreement opera already accommodates a wide variety of vocal styles. The problem is cultural rather than merely stylistic. The fear is often expressed that opera has become a museum category, under which a restricted (and in fact quite small) repertoire of works by dead composers is supplemented only by a few difficult new works, of which virtually none survive their first production. This last point in itself is nothing new. At various times in which opera has flourished, such as in the nineteenth-century heyday of Italian opera, hundreds of works have been staged and never revived. The difference is that, as is generally the case with popular forms in which most works are expected to be disposable, the investment of resources was relatively low compared with what is now involved in staging a new opera. Above all, the composer's investment of effort in any one work was less. The Wagnerian model of the heroic composer creating a unique and challenging masterpiece will work only on the rare occasions that this is indeed what is created, and it cannot sustain a practice or tradition. A few twentieth-century composers have tried to deal with this problem, but their experiments have not had continuing results. Weill, in his collaboration with Brecht, worked in music theatre outside the opera house. Benjamin Britten, who was comparatively prolific among twentieth-century opera composers, deliberately aimed in some of his works at an effect simpler than that of his first (and still most successful) opera, the very traditional *Peter Grimes*, and in the 'church parables' looked to a staging that would avoid the theatre.

The fact that the operatic repertoire is small, old and not expanding does not mean that this repertoire itself has only a small or 'élitist' audience; that complaint is also made, but it is to an increasing extent untrue. The opera house may be a museum, but museums are themselves popular. The problem is not so much that the tradition of opera is cut off from popular appreciation, as that new pieces of musical theatre which are unselfconsciously enjoyed by many people are cut off from the tradition of opera, and so from what makes opera uniquely interesting, the achievement of intense dramatic expression by essentially musical means. Cultural critics such as Adorno saw this development as an historical inevitability, but despair over the future of interesting musical theatre is uncalled for. There will perhaps be new works that will cut through current anxieties and make these definitional complexities out of date. What they will be cannot of course be foreseen, except by someone who will write one.

Words, music, drama

The relations of speech and song are a problem only for some operas, but all opera has to find an accommodation between words and music. Dr Burney wrote in the 1780s,

As the British government consists of three estates: King, Lords, and Commons, so an opera in its first institution consisted of Poetry, Music and Machinery: but as politicians have observed, that the balance of power is frequently disturbed by some one of the three estates encroaching upon the other two, so one of these three constituent parts of a musical drama generally preponderates, at the expence of the other two. In the first operas POETRY seems to have been the most important personage; but about the middle of the last century MACHINERY and

DECORATION seemed to take the lead ... But as the art of singing and dramatic composition improved, MUSIC took the lead.

Burney's words are carefully chosen to avoid the false idea that the balance of power between music and words is the same thing as a balance between music and *drama*. It is a fallacy to argue that since, in a musical drama, the music obviously provides the music, so the words must provide the drama. As anyone knows who has ever enjoyed an opera, music and words both provide the drama. In the terms of Burney's political analogy, the drama is the government itself, rather than one of the estates. Yet it has proved easy to forget this, particularly on the various occasions when it has been thought that through some imbalance opera had become undramatic and stood in need of reform.

Dr Johnson's celebrated description of opera as 'an exotic and irrational entertainment' was directed to the Italian opera of his time, above all to *opera seria* with its lengthy *da capo* arias, which imposed an elaborate musical structure, were not intended to secure any dramatic development in the course of the song itself, and greatly emphasised musical decorations which gave singers an opportunity for technical display. As well as implying certain musical and dramatic forms, *opera seria* also involved a set of rigid theatrical conventions, under which, for instance, a singer expected to exit at the end of his or her aria.

Opera seria was so effectively ridiculed (notably in *The Beggar's Opera*, the success of which induced Handel to move towards freer forms), so eloquently criticised, and so creatively replaced, that it has stood for almost two centuries as a paradigm of ways in which an operatic style may fail to realise the potentialities of sung drama. The lack of performances mirrors the reputation: leaving aside the special case of *La clemenza di Tito* (which in any case departs from the conventions), no *opera seria* holds the stage, even though Handel's, in particular, contain much outstanding music.* The seeming finality of this historical judgment on *opera seria* has perhaps discouraged discussion of what exactly was wrong with it. The standard criticism is that it is 'static' or 'undramatic', but such terms do no more than register what needs to be explained. *Opera seria* did not, as the criticisms may imply, simply ignore the relations of music and words to

---

*This essay was published before the more recent experiments in the staging of Handel, but see pp. 76, 123–5 and 130 for later references to *Theodora*.

drama; it approached them, rather, in a special way, and if, having taken that way, it seems now to lie in irreversible coma, it is instructive to ask why that should be.

Dr Burney (in a different work) used his preferred terms of the division of labour to describe the war between the tradition of *opera seria* and Gluck's 'reform' operas:

> Party runs as high among poets, musicians and their adherents, at Vienna as elsewhere. Metastasio and Hasse may be said to be at the head of one of the principal sects; and Calsabigi and Gluck of another. The first, regarding all innovations as quackery, adhere to the ancient form of the musical drama, in which the poet and the musician claim equal attention from the audience; the bard in the recitatives and the narrative parts; and the composer in the airs, duos, and choruses. The second party depend more on theatrical effects, propriety of character, simplicity of diction, and of musical execution, than on, what *they* style, flowery descriptions, superfluous similes, sententious and cold morality, on one side, with tiresome symphonies, and long divisions, on the other.

Calzabigi, who as librettist and propagandist was a prime mover of the reform associated with *Orfeo* and other later works of Gluck, himself wrote of the new style,

> All is nature here, all is passion; there are no sententious reflections, no philosophy or politics, no paragons of virtue . . . [The plot is] reduced to the dimensions of Greek tragedy, and therefore has the unique advantage of exciting terror and compassion in the same way as spoken tragedy . . . The music has no other function than to express what arises from the words, which are therefore neither smothered by notes nor used to lengthen the spectacle unduly, because it is ridiculous to prolong the sentence 'I love you' (for instance) with a hundred notes when nature has restricted it to three.

Each of these texts may give the impression that the reform party's aim was to redress the balance in favour of words as against music; and since the reform party not only won their war against *opera seria*, but are likely to be understood now as urging in their own time a message about musical drama that is rather the same as Wagner's or Verdi's in the next century, we may well ourselves see the reform in those same terms. But it is not an adequate account of what the reformers themselves wanted, and even less so of what modern taste may find lacking in o*pera seria.* The *da capo* aria was not emotionally inexpressive, and the emotions it expressed (at its best, very effectively) were relevant to the action. Moreover, it cannot be an objection to those arias or to the other conventions of this style that the music is not evenly directed to the onward movement of the action. That is true in some way of almost all operas, and in an opera with self-contained arias it is standard that they should not move the action forward in time, but deepen it psychologically.

The peculiarity of the *da capo* arias lay, rather, in the fact that, by a well-established rhetorical decorum, each aria was allowed to express only one emotion. In addition, the words, having established what the emotion was, could be used decoratively for musical, or at least vocal, purposes, with the repetitions and the elongations of syllables about which Calzabigi complained. To a later taste, the very idea of identifying and labelling the emotions in the way that this tradition required is likely to seem schematic and unsatisfactory. Later Italian opera, particularly in the hands of Verdi, can of course wonderfully express very simple emotions, but then the means of expression themselves are, or seem, very direct. In *opera seria,* what are labelled as very simple feelings receive an elaborate musical expression; the complexity of the musical means is not matched by any complication of feeling or psychological development. The power of the music, though it can be considerable, is, so to speak, earthed by the simplicity of the dramatic content and the determined labelling effected by the text.

The difficulties with *opera seria* cannot be captured in terms of the relative importance of words and music; nor by the charge – which is in good part untrue – that the form was emotionally inexpressive. The reformers themselves spoke in praise of the simple and the natural as contrasted with the complex and artificial. In part, this merely represented the Rousseauesque fashion of the time, and certainly the lesson could not be drawn that the way for opera to succeed where *opera seria* had failed was just by being simpler – the technical innocence of Gluck was not in itself the sign-post pointing towards Mozart. The basic point was rather that the elaboration of means in *opera seria* was not well related to its emotional and dramatic content. The music was too complex for the content, but equally the content was too simple for the music. Above all, the style did not adequately acknowledge the power of music to express feeling that cannot be fully captured in words, a power which underlies the special opportunities that opera possesses as a form of drama. Those possibilities are not, of course, a more recent discovery, but are exploited by some of the earliest operas, notably by Monteverdi.

Some of the limitations of *opera seria* were implicit in its forms, but it was also true that it suffered from having ceded (not for the last time in the history of opera) too much control to the performers, whose demands could impede both the composer and the librettist. Wagner shrewdly said that Gluck's reforms did not really advance the dramatist in relation to the composer, but the composer in relation to the singers, a remark which itself implies that if the older form was undramatic, it was not because the music was emphasised at the expense of the words. The innovations that Wagner himself preached in his writings claimed to reassert a balance between the elements of opera, but some of the terms that he used do not express very satisfactorily what was most radical in his practice (or, rather, his constantly developing practice) in the works from *Das Rheingold* on. He sometimes expressed his aspirations in terms of the *Gesamtkunstwerk*, a drama that would bind into a total unity music, words, acting and stage spectacle. As critics have pointed out, this conception in itself determines very little. Every opera puts these elements together in one way or another, and indeed a kind of opera that Wagner peculiarly despised, the French grand opera of Scribe and Meyerbeer (of which he memorably said that it consisted of effects without causes), could claim in one sense to offer a more 'total' work of art than his, since it standardly included ballet, which his typically did not. The theory of the *Gesamtkunstwerk* did not in itself fully reveal how the relations of words, music and the visual were to be adapted to what Wagner really wanted, which was a new conception not just of opera but of drama.

Wagner regarded French opera as bombastically empty, distinguished neither for its words nor for its music. Rossini, the master of Italian opera, he saw as a counter-revolutionary, comparing him to a reactionary statesman: 'As Metternich, with perfect logic on his side, could not conceive the state under any form but that of absolute monarchy, so Rossini, with no less force of argument, could conceive the opera under no other form than that of absolute melody.' In this context, and granted also that he thought that the genius of Mozart had been poured into inadequate texts (and, in the case of *Così fan tutte*, a deplorable subject), Wagner particularly emphasised the importance of the words – which, for all his operas, were of course his own words. In developing his later style, he at first tended to assert the *primacy* of words, and *Das Rheingold*, in particular, is to some extent an expression of this ideal. However, as the music of the *Ring* developed, and in the light of his experience with *Tristan* and *Die Meistersinger* he gave up this emphasis. The words were always of course important; he invested them with a complex philosophical content, removed almost all repetitions, and did his best to make the text heard over the music, placing the orchestra in the Festspielhaus at Bayreuth under the stage (though he chose this arrangement also because he wanted there to be an uninterrupted view of the stage picture). But while the force of the words was essential, he moved to a view that if anything was primary, it was the music: in a later essay, he described his dramas as 'deeds of music made manifest'. The sheer cumulative progression of the work almost inevitably meant that the music should become more complex as the drama went on, and in addition to that, the technical developments in his style during the period in which he broke off from the cycle produced an alteration in the music, in particular a symphonic flexibility in the use of the motives, which is very evident at the beginning of the third act of *Siegfried*, the point at which he took it up again.

Time, expression and the inner world

Perhaps the single most powerful resource of opera as a dramatic form is its capacity to use musical means not only to advance the action in time, but to deepen it. It implies a complex relation between real and dramatic time; while time passes in the theatre, a sequence is unfolded by the orchestra and singers which does not represent a sequence at all, or at least not a sequence of events, but some other dimension of the action, often a state of mind, a mood or a motivation. The arias in *opera seria*, it has already been suggested, were a device for exploring the emotional implications of the action, but it was not entirely successful, partly because of a restrictive rhetoric of the emotions, partly because the parts in which the action was advanced were schematic and compressed and often without musical interest.

In Mozart and Da Ponte's comedies, the resource is developed in many different and very subtle ways. It is used to distinguish the characters from one another; moreover, it is deployed differently in the various operas, and this contributes significantly to their distinctive atmospheres. In *The Marriage of Figaro*, each principal character has at least one self-revelatory aria, and these differ not only in what they say and in their musical character, but in their occasion. Both Figaro and the Count burst into declaration of their feelings in the face of immediate events, but the Countess needs no special occasion, and when we first see her, she is overflowing with nostalgia and regret. In *Don Giovanni* it is important that, while other characters sing about themselves, Giovanni never does. He is all action, and the lack of any piece that reveals anything more about him leaves us with a very appropriate sense that there is nothing to be revealed; his significance lies in such things as the vitality that he, in his music, communicates to everyone else. *Così fan tutte* uses to contrasting effect declarations made by the same characters at different stages of the action. It creates the remarkable impression that the elaborate conventional arias in the first act are public performances, occurring in real time, while the expressions of feeling later in the work, particularly from Fiordiligi, come from an inner world; just for this reason, when the tenor interrupts her most affecting piece, 'Fra gli amplessi', the sense is given that he has broken not just into her song but into her life.

In Wagner's work, the resources of psychological exploration became the essence of musical drama. This was not altogether his intention. He wanted his works to constitute a new kind of myth, a modern analogue to Aeschylean tragedy. To some extent, he succeeded, but it was perhaps inevitable that in the nineteenth century these aims should be shaped by explorations of the subjective individual consciousness. Particularly in the *Ring*, mythic, symbolic and political themes are arranged in a structure of personal motivation which in itself could well figure in a more naturalistic style of drama. The means that Wagner invented to make this possible are to be found in a text and a musical texture that make it very easy to move between the inner and the outer world: exchanges between characters, first-personal declarations made by one character to another, and music or words which express a welling up of the characters' conscious or unconscious thoughts merge into one another in a fluent and natural way. At the same time, the flow of these materials is controlled by a powerful sense of theatrical pace. Critics of Wagner's works (who include some who hate them, with an intensity probably unique in operatic taste) are disposed to say that they are too long, but this is the consequence of dislike, not its ground: since the works are long, those who hate them naturally find them too long. Some passages can be recognised even by enthusiasts as unnecessary (though it is not easy to get agreement on which they are), but none of the mature works is seriously too long for what it is trying to do, and in all of them, well performed, there is a steady pulse against which the developments of both the inner and the outer life unfold in a timely and coherent way.

The contrasts in almost all respects between Wagner and Verdi are so sharp that in general there is not much to be learned from them about the aesthetics of opera. The fact that two musical geniuses, born in the same year, should produce works so totally different in their aims and methods is, certainly, revealing about two national cultures. Verdi took up a popular tradition of opera, and insisted that he remained within it, as he developed works of increasing complexity and technical sophistication. It is entirely fitting that at his funeral the large crowd should have spontaneously started to sing 'Va pensiero', the famous patriotic chorus from *Nabucco*, his first masterpiece, written nearly sixty years before. Verdi was a national hero, and he was popular in the straightforward sense that his tunes could be taken up by the town band, the café trio or the barrel organ. The contrast with Wagner's artistic relations to nationalism, and with his conception of 'a people', could not be more striking. Wagner wanted to give the German people a German art. This implied both that they did not yet have such a thing, and that a creative individual was needed to bring it into being. Moreover, this creative act was to occur at the frontiers of expressive innovation. The work that more than any other Wagner acknowledged as his inspiration was Beethoven's Ninth Symphony, and his ambitions were defined in terms of the self-consciously progressive art work. Verdi merely ignored any such ideas for most of his career, and treated them with great suspicion when in his later years they were pressed on him by Boito.

Granted these vast differences, comparisons between the two composers are often uninteresting. In the handling of dramatic time, however, the diametrical differences between them are instructive. Verdi was always concerned to achieve pace, constantly urging his librettists to cut and condense, and his works are marked by a powerful forward movement, very characteristic of him and not simply of the Italian tradition (there is a marked contrast with Bellini). The pace is that of external events; his characters are almost always doing something, and their psychology is expressed typically in action rather than in reflection. Some of his operas, above all *Rigoletto*, achieve a perfect dramatic pace in these terms: rapid developments are rapidly unfolded, with no sense of theatrical strain. He had other ways, as well, of handling dramatic pace. Two of his finest works offer a very satisfactory sense of elapsed time, but in interestingly different terms: *Don Carlos* is slower and more reflective, and leaves a greater space for the exploration of motive, while *Falstaff* sustains a very fast pace adjusted to comic developments, and does it by using a radically original and fluent musical idiom.

There are other Verdi operas, however, in which the effect of his brisk dealings with time is more questionable, and they include some which in other respects are among his finest. Just because the inner life of his characters is given very largely through the events presented, there is a danger that as the presentation of the events speeds up, so, seemingly, does their inner life: we may be left with no sense of a space beside or among the happenings in which we can locate their thoughts or feelings. There is a problem of this kind in the second act of *La traviatar*, where the narration is so briskly compressed that the hero and the heroine both seem to be acting in a state of frantic haste. There is not much to encourage the thought that this effect is intended, and the impression can be distinctly like that of watching an old film.

A similar difficulty, at a deeper level, affects *Otello*. Boito is often complimented for having eliminated the first act of Shakespeare's play, but that act in fact lays the basis of the relations between the main characters, and its removal, together with the compression of time in which Othello's feelings change, moves his character sharply towards the pathological. In addition, within the tight boundaries set by the compression, Boito could find no room for the already difficult matter of Iago's motivation, and tried to condense it into one self-revelatory monologue, the famous 'Credo', which produced a magnificent aria but also contributed to making the situation less humanly credible. In the case of *Otello*, considerations of speed, more than anything else, serve to turn a tragedy into a melodrama.

The extraordinary success of Wagner's manipulation of the relations between outer action and inner feeling had its own cost. Because every aspect of the characters' experience is expressed and nourished by the unified flow of musical material, which in each work has its own distinctive quality, there is a danger that the characters will seem to merge – at the limit, that the whole may seem to belong to one experience. If this goes too far, the spectator's experience of the drama may take on the quality of being inside the composer's head: it is related to the feeling of being consumed or absorbed which is a well-known reaction to Wagner's work, and which is notoriously feared and resented by many who experience it. It is a kind of reaction inconceivable in the case of Mozart or of Verdi, where there is no tendency for the power and individuality of the style to threaten the seeming autonomy of the characters.

Debussy had this kind of difficulty in mind in setting out to write a post-Wagnerian opera. It was not merely what he called the 'American opulence' of Wagner's textures that he wanted to escape. Harmonically *Pelléas et Mélisande* owes a good deal to the experiments of *Parsifal*, but it conceives the relations of music and drama in terms very different from Wagner's. 'I do not feel tempted to imitate what I admire in Wagner,' Debussy wrote; 'my conception of dramatic art is different. According to mine, music begins where speech fails. Music is intended to convey the inexpressible . . . I would have her always discreet.' This in itself might seem to fit a traditional view of *Pelléas*, that it achieves its great refinement at the cost of an enervated passivity, an image of it which is encouraged if one is too impressed by Debussy's admiration for Poe and his recurrent interest in *The Fall of the House of Usher*. But Debussy also said that what he wanted for libretti were 'poems that will provide me with changing scenes, varied as regards place and atmosphere, in which the characters will not argue, but live their lives and work out their destinies'. Joseph Kerman has described *Pelléas* as a 'sung play', and this arrives at the same point, from the opposite direction, as Mallarmé's remark about Maeterlinck's drama when it first appeared, that it was an opera without music. The music does not cancel the work's character as a drama, or impose passivity on it. What it emphasises, rather, is the imperfection of action, and human beings' indeterminate understanding of what they are doing. 'Nous ne voyons jamais que l'envers des destinées,' the aged Arkel remarks, 'l'envers même de la nôtre': the back, or reverse side, of our lives. We do see something, but it is the wrong way round and fragmentary, gaining a sense only from another point of view. Debussy presents this compelling picture of the mental world in a way uniquely successful in opera. He laid aside every convention by which opera had traditionally been assumed to express the inner life of its characters explicitly, totally, and on the authority of the composer.

Pelléas is particularly difficult to produce; it is hard to embody its basic sense of the indeterminacy of human relations, and of there simply being no truth of the kind that the jealous Golaud seeks. Pressed in one direction, it dissolves into a faintly Symbolist vagueness, while in the other it offers a rather nasty but underdescribed domestic disaster. But its difficulties also measure its achievement, as being one of the few operas to have engaged with the typically twentieth-century idea that reality is not merely given, but both demands interpretation and can defeat it. Some works of Richard Strauss flirt with such ideas – *Ariadne auf Naxos* perhaps, or *Capriccio* – but none is committed to developing them. Stravinsky, in *The Rake's Progress*, characteristically changed the subject, and self-consciously addressed the technical problems of a less self-conscious operatic tradition.

The one composer besides Debussy whose operas successfully took up typically modern problems of psychological opacity and the dramatist's narrative authority was Berg. He is a descendant of Wagner not just in technical terms of the history of atonality, but as one who created a new kind of musical drama from demandingly avant-garde materials. He resembles Wagner, too, in an insistent (in his case, obsessional) compositorial presence, but he avoided the problem that Wagner had left, of reconciling that presence with the characters' autonomy, by cultivating a dramatic effect in which any appearance of that autonomy has disappeared. His characters lack effective action, or an inner life, or both. The protagonists of the two operas are victims, and almost every other character (with the exceptions of Marie in *Wozzeck* and Geschwitz in *Lulu*) is a grotesque and empty construct of behaviour. The conventional name of this style, 'Expressionism', may well have been applied to it by an imperfect analogy with painting, but it has its logic in the history of music. An operatic technique which restricts characters to depersonalised aspects of a compelling and disturbing musical development is directly descended, through Schoenberg's experiments, from Wagner's design of expressing the rich inner life of his characters by making it immediately accessible to their musical environment. This design contains the possibility, which is already present in *Tristan* and is most obvious in Amfortas's music in *Parsifal*, that the expression will itself become the environment. The distinctions dissolve between the characters' inner life and the whole world of the opera, and that part of Wagner's project which consisted in finding new musical means to represent individual psychological character (in itself, a traditional aim) falls away.

Performance and repetition

There are a few plays that are constantly revived, and they are almost all masterpieces, frequently performed because they are thought to reward repeated reinterpretation. There are many pieces of music of which the same is true, but there are more which do not make the same claim to inexhaustible depth, yet are frequently performed because people wish simply to hear them, or to hear a particular artist perform them. In this respect, musical drama is music rather than drama. Some of the works in the repertoire do fall into the class of inexhaustible masterpieces, but more do not, and they are repeatedly performed because of an interest in performance rather than in dramatic reinterpretation.

The interest in performance is in the first place an interest in singers, and there are some people whose concern with opera is primarily directed to the talents and achievements of singers. As well as discriminating connoisseurs, there are devoted and enthusiastic fans who attach themselves to leading artists. Their popularity can give these artists great power in the opera house, and the demands, tantrums and absurdities of some performers in the past are legendary. This is less to be found now, and there are probably no singers left who insist, as some used to do, on wearing their own costume in a given role whatever the production might be. Gluck, Verdi and others opposed such excesses in their time, and in the last fifty years, particularly under Wagnerian influence, the dramatic demands of opera have to a great extent prevailed against the tastes and habits of more traditional performers and their supporters. The development has brought about a great improvement in operatic acting, and it has also yielded many radically new and interesting productions.

It is true that the idiosyncrasies of singers have to some extent been replaced by those of directors, and most seasoned opera-goers have seen in recent decades some production of a well-known work in which only the music revealed what opera it was. This is not only a matter of a fashionable trend; it also involves a shift in what is meant by the repetition of operas. When the emphasis moves to dramatic realisation, a new staging of an opera cannot count as simply a new series of performances, but is an invitation to a reinterpretation. However, since many operas that are worth performing offer few rewards to dramatic rediscovery, attempts to find new significance in their drama can be very strained. In an extreme case, the enterprise may be thought to be based on a misunderstanding, a confusion between an exploration of a work and, simply, a performance of it. But there is no easy road back from this point. A merely conventional production may well be disappointing unless the performance is very good indeed, and the growing popularity of opera, which means more performances, joins, rather paradoxically, with increasing dramatic demands on the works performed, with the effect that the already small repertoire becomes even more restricted. The next demand on directors' ingenuity may be to invent ways in which dramatically less interesting operas can be merely performed.

The historical conflicts between the dramatic and the performance aspects of opera have been concerned with the power of singers. They do not call in question the power of singing, which is at the heart of all opera. The enjoyment of opera, particularly of Italian opera, immediately involves the enjoyment of a technique. At a fine operatic performance, the audience is conscious of the singers' achievement and the presence of physical style and vitality; a feeling of performance and of the performers' artistry is more constantly at the front of the mind than it is with other dramatic arts. It is because of this that outbreaks of applause may be appropriate, though the granting of encores is a lot less common than it once was. These practices may sometimes get in the way of the drama, but the sense of performance in itself does not; it is allied with musical intensity in reinforcing the drama. There are interesting comparisons in these respects with ballet, where the sense of performance and technique is paramount, but which (in Western culture at least) is less committed to being a dramatic art, and has closer relations with both the decorative and the athletic. At the same time, the demands on opera singers, even more than on other musical performers, are not altogether unlike those on athletes, and high-risk aspects of physical performance uniquely combine in the case of opera with possibilities of dramatic expression to make it an exceptionally difficult enterprise, and all the more powerful when it goes well.

W. H. Auden said that 'in a sense, there can be no tragic opera', because singing in itself too evidently seems a free and enjoyable activity: 'the singer may be playing the role of a deserted bride who is about to kill herself, but we feel quite certain as we listen that not only we, but also she, is having a wonderful time'. The judgment about tragedy might be disputed, but Auden's remark contains an important truth about the aesthetics of opera. Particularly in the Italian style, it presents its audience immediately with musical artistry and achievement, and so, more generally, with an obvious

artifice – conventions of musical form and performance that are not transparent, as blank verse can sometimes be, but constantly manifest. Because
of this, there is a particular technique available to the operatic composer,
which is that of securing an effect through the audience's consciousness
that this is what is happening. A theatrical device is made to work, not by
concealing it, but by securing the audience's complicity in it. This technique is not peculiar to opera, but it is specially important to it, and its
importance is connected to the point that operas do not have to have
dramatic or musical depth in order to be worth seeing over and over
again. When one sees an effective opera again, not because it is the kind
of work that one might understand more deeply on further experience of
it, but just because one wants to see a good performance, its enjoyment
at the level of drama is often increased by this sense of familiarity, of
seeing the wheels of artifice turn.

The master of this technique is Puccini. He is an immensely popular
opera composer, and his works are staged by every opera house. He had
outstanding melodic gifts and was a notably inventive orchestrator. The
libretti of his operas (several by Giacosa and Illica) are ingeniously
constructed. Yet his critical reputation is not as unqualified as his success,
and many, while acknowledging his achievement, find it hard to dismiss a
distinct sense of the cynical and the manipulative about it. All his major
works are sentimental or melodramatic or both, and while 'melodrama',
etymologically speaking, is what all opera must be, the term in fact carries
a limiting sense which, in Puccini's case, is compounded by the fact that
the melodrama is not at all innocent. His consciousness that he came at
the end of a long tradition, together with the taste for cruelty which he
himself called his 'Neronian instinct', means that *Tosca* or *Madam Butterfly*
is a very long way from *Un ballo in maschera*. It is hard to think of a parallel
in any other art to enduring works that are at once as effective and as
dubious as these. The secret of their working so well is that their skill and
their very self-consciousness play into the audience's experience of opera
as performance. In enjoying these familiar works, part of the pleasure lies
in the sense of seeing Puccini do the trick again. In relying so ingeniously
on this sense, he was exploiting something that is inherent to some degree
in the performance of any opera, and that is why his talent, suspect as it is,
is true to the nature of the form.

The case of Puccini, and the relation of his achievements to opera as
performance, are important for the aesthetics of opera. In his path-breaking

work of opera criticism, *Opera as Drama,* Joseph Kerman was particularly and quotably scathing about *Tosca* as he was also about *Der Rosenkavalier.* It is certainly important for the critic to mark off these triumphant examples of, respectively, sensationalism and kitsch from such works as *The Marriage of Figaro* or *Tristan* or *Don Carlos.* Yet it is probable that *Tosca* and *Der Rosenkavalier* will be popular with opera lovers as long as there are opera-lovers, and rightly so. If they are not unqualifiedly masterpieces, they are masterpieces of opera. It is very characteristic of opera that this should be possible. Because opera is musical drama, some of its works can bring these resources together to achieve a power unsurpassed in the dramatic arts. At the same time, opera is musical performance, and this does not merely have its consequences for the practice of opera-going, for the loyalties of its audience, and for the kinds of interest that enthusiasts can appropriately take in it. It has its own implications for the opportunities that opera can offer its creators.

Bibliography

Auden, W. H., 'Notes on Music and Opera', in *The Dyer's Hand* (London, 1963)
Auden, W. H., 'The World of Opera', in *Secondary Worlds* (London, 1969)
Burney, Charles, *The Present State of Music in Germany* (London, 1775)
Burney, Charles, *General History of Music,* 4 vols (London, 1782–9)
Kerman, Joseph, O*pera as Drama* (New York, 1956)
Kivy, Peter, *Osmin's Rage: Philosophical Reflections on Opera, Drama and Text* (Princeton, 1988)
Robinson, Peter, *Opera and Ideas: From Mozart to Strauss* (New York, 1985)
Wagner, Richard, writings on music and drama, see the references in the notes to chapter 9, 'Wagner and the Transcendence of Politics'

2

Mozart's Comedies and the Sense
of an Ending

It is not easy to bring a serious dramatic comedy to its end. A well-written farce ends itself – the last combination of pieces is reached, the acceleration gets to its limit, the play stops. But a comedy may well face a problem raised by its own depth. It may have expressed or suggested feelings of considerable intensity, and embodied them in happenings which are at any rate unusual; at the same time it is related to, and belongs to, a normal world. The plot has its shape, which is closed when the play ends, but one must be allowed to believe that the characters go on. In farce, at the end the characters are folded up and put away. In tragedy, characteristically, when it is finished, it is all finished: if the characters continue at all, they do not continue into anything – it was *another* tragedy that provided Oedipus the King with a future, and with an eventual end of his own. In comedy, the characters live, and also live on.

The end should not anticipate the future too insistently, or the shape of the work is lost, and the time of its closing can seem arbitrary, like closing time. Comedy may bring to bear on its closing moments recollection, a felt condensation, of what has happened; those moments are also a beginning, but one which is different from others in virtue of what has just happened. A particular sense of that is given by Shakespeare, whose comedies end often in the melancholy of departures, of the characters going in different directions.

The resources of music do not necessarily make the problems of meeting these demands any easier for an operatic comedy. The mere fact that its end is the end of a musical piece, and the normal expectation that such a work will end with an extremely positive and emphatic coda, has the effect of closing the opera from succeeding time. Since in opera the life of the characters is in the music, the invitation, essential to comedy, to imagine a continuation of their lives can be frustrated by the impossibility (or at any rate the inappropriateness) of imagining some more music.

In two, at least, of his three great Italian comedies, Mozart presented himself with these difficulties in a particularly acute form; and even the subtlety and boldness that he brought to them have not left their endings beyond question. In *Don Giovanni* and *Così fan tutte*, the end has often been seen as the problem. However, if there is a problem, in each case, that cannot be the full extent of it – it must reach back into understanding the work as a whole.

It is significant that there is no comparable question with *Die Zauberflöte*. If there are problems about that opera, they have nothing to do with the way in which it ends: a static celebratory chorus of praise and thanksgiving is an entirely proper end to that drama, if that is what it is. There is a revealing contrast in this with *Fidelio*, which similarly ends *with* music rather than *in* it, but which leaves one with the strong impression that the emotional structure embodied in the music is shaped differently from the drama, and indeed lasts longer than the drama does.

In Mozart's Italian comedies, there is no question of that. The dramatic significance of each of these works extends to its end, and the ultimate finale displays that same expression of dramatic development through complex musical forms which Mozart exploits throughout these works, especially in the finales of earlier acts (including, in the case *of Don Giovanni*, the extra finale which actually occurs, on the plan eventually adopted, in the middle of the second act).

The Romantic taste which saw Don Giovanni himself as a Faustian or Promethean figure defying the cosmic order notoriously found the final fugato sextet of the opera unnecessary, and limiting to the heroic drama. The sextet is in truth, as all modern productions acknowledge, absolutely essential, as defining – in a sense – a 'return to normal', something which itself helps to define the meaning of previous events and of Giovanni himself. In fact, the characters, with the exception of Zerlina and Masetto, scarcely do 'return to normal', but rather try to stick something together from what is left now that Giovanni is gone. In particular, they are not simply operating in a space left for virtue now that vice has been punished. Life without Giovanni will be life that has lost a very powerful and single-minded embodiment of qualities which are indeed human, even though he himself lacked several important aspects of humanity.

The closing bars have to define the boundary between the extraordinary events of the drama, including the extraordinary figure of Giovanni himself, and the world of everyone else, and it is fundamental that they define it in a way which does not exclude him from what makes ordinary life worth living. Giovanni's own end and the end of the opera both affirm that there is no actual human life that can be lived as unconditionally as his, but, at the same time, they recognise that any vitality that other people have must sustain the dream of being as free from conditions as his was.

Don Giovanni might be said to draw the boundary between the extraordinary and the ordinary as a line between nature and convention. But it is not any arbitrary convention that constitutes the ordinary, but the general idea of convention that is necessary to human nature, and which provides a possible human life. In *Così fan tutte*, however, the end seems to represent a return to convention of a much shallower kind, which involves rejecting a developing and 'natural' sentiment, that of the girls for their substitute lovers, which we have been led by Mozart to take seriously in a series of effective and increasingly expressive pieces, culminating in the beautiful and distressing episode of 'Fra gli amplessi'. After we have been led, very carefully, through all this, and the desires and demands presented in it have been acknowledged, everyone is briskly, indeed brutally, returned to a conventional arrangement which was grounded, as we were equally carefully shown, in shallower sentiments.

Some critics – perhaps most of those who have seen that *Così* is a deeper and stranger work than it seems, and that there is a problem about how to read it – have seen its ending as a failure, as the point at which the lack of fit cannot be concealed between what Da Ponte wrote and what Mozart made of it. On this view, the end was originally intended to represent a return from fancy or unreason or extravagance to reason and reality, but it does not work, either because Mozart did not see it that way, or because we, two hundred years later, cannot see it that way and can understand it only as a cruel return from reality and freedom to convention and domination. It would follow that it is a work flawed either by its creators or by time, and, either way, the end of it does not acceptably draw the line between what happens in the opera and the world of ordinary relations.

On another view, no-one has made a mistake, and the affirmation that convention is reality and that deeper sentiment will be overruled is exactly what the work means. Its bitterness will then be considerable, and it will be compressed into the end – compressed, indeed, into the *fact* of the end, since there is little material in the closing bars actually to express it. Peter Hall has almost brought off this conception of *Così* in his Glyndebourne production, in which the characters at the end look like the stunned occupants of a wedding photograph.

Così, as it now seems to us, does leave indeterminate exactly what boundary is being drawn at its end, and what exactly counts, after all this, as the normal and as the irregular. That, on any showing, leaves some problem about the end, a problem which perhaps ultimately dissolves in the recognition that the feeling of discomfort with which we are left by the ambiguities of this work is itself entirely appropriate to its subject.

Even the end of *Figaro* may be thought to raise a difficulty, though its existence, so far as I know, was first suggested by a critic who does not regard it as a difficulty at all, but as a perfection. Joseph Kerman has written of the beautiful Andante chorus of forgiveness which holds the action still before the very last moments that 'the reconciliation of the Count and Countess is deep and true, the most beautiful thing in the opera', and that this looks forward to *Die Zauberflöte* and to the heights of consciousness appropriate to a noble hero and heroine. If this is what this music had to mean, then there would be a problem, since that is not true of the Count and Countess, and we cannot be required at the very last moment of the drama suddenly to believe it. Nothing has basically changed with the Count and the Countess, nor, even at this instant, are they very close together: they may be seeing more than usual, but they are doing so apart. The day's doings have probably left the Countess's loneliness very much where it was. Our straightforward reaction to the opera, that it is in Figaro and Susanna that some larger and more spontaneous humanity triumphs, is surely right.

The Act IV finale of *Figaro* is indeed perfect, and that passage is essential to it. What is important is the calm, the moment of complete understanding, between what has happened and what we are allowed to believe will yet happen. It centres on the Count and Countess, and could not centre on anyone else, but there is no problem in the fact that we cannot believe in their permanent reconciliation, because insofar as the passage looks backwards and forwards, it is not simply about them. It rather brings the whole range of feeling of the 'folle journée' into a momentary condensation, before everyone moves on into the next and more ordinary day. At the end of *Figaro*, the difficult task of marking a boundary between the shape of a comedy and the world to which it belongs is solved at a deeper level and with more perfect assurance than in any other opera.

3

Mozart's *Figaro*

A Question of Class?

About ten weeks after the first performance of *The Marriage of Figaro* in 1786, a Vienna paper carried this paragraph: 'What is not allowed to be said these days is sung, one may say, with *Figaro* – this piece, which was prohibited in Paris and not allowed to be performed here as a comedy, either in a bad or in a good translation, we have at last had the felicity to see represented as an opera. It will be seen that we are doing better than the French.' That paragraph suggests only that on the musical stage Mozart and Da Ponte could get away with things not permitted to Beaumarchais' original play; but it is not far from that to the idea that the opera is actually more innocuous than the play, and avoided scandal by avoiding being scandalous. A few years later, in fact, a Berlin paper could say that it was Mozart's music alone that could make this 'capon-ised' *Figaro* tolerable, 'so much has he suffered from the mutilation'.

Right from the beginning there has been a conception, one still widely held, that Beaumarchais wrote a politically radical play which Da Ponte and Mozart turned, indeed, into a masterpiece, but a masterpiece of sentiment, sensuality and individual character, devoid of political or socially critical content. For some this is a pity, for many more it is not; but for both it is a fact.

But is it a fact? This is the question I want to look at. The truth, even about Beaumarchais, is more complicated than the usual story makes out.

Beaumarchais certainly had his problems with the censors and with Louis XVI himself, who first said that the piece would never be played; but after some successful intrigue by Beaumarchais, which attracted useful publicity for the play, it was put on with vast success at the Comédie-Française in April 1784 and continued to play to delighted houses. 'They have laughed at their own expense,' said the Baronne d'Oberkirch of the aristocratic audience, 'and what is worse, have made others laugh. They will regret it, later on.' But even if the Baronne was right about the eventual effect, it was not, in fact, the distinctively political content of the play that had caused its troubles, or caused trouble to its German translation later in Vienna. The objection to the play was not primarily that it was subversive, but that it was indecent; it was seen as licentious, with regard to such things as the Countess's relations with Cherubino – an element, incidentally, later to be admired by French critics as among the most original in the piece.

Beaumarchais' reputation as a subversive writer increased with hindsight, and in the 1860s Alexandre Dumas *fils* could overexcitedly describe him, on the strength of *The Marriage of Figaro*, as a 'revolutionary writer'. But the play was not so perceived at the time, and it is not easy to find all that much explicit comment in it to invite the description. There are some remarks about politicians and the administration of justice; and Figaro's monologue in the last act includes sour jokes about the privileges of rank and the workings of censorship; but even in that case, which is sometimes thought the prime example of the change from social resentment in the play to purely individual feeling in the opera, even there the differences can easily be exaggerated – Beaumarchais, too, uses as his guiding thread sexual jealousy. The main difference is rather that Beaumarchais' Figaro (in whose autobiographical ramblings Sainte-Beuve detected a touch of the club bore) never comes near the depths of hurt and bitterness that Mozart uncovered in the recitative 'Tutto è disposto', and the snaking unsettled aria which follows it. But is radical comment necessarily a matter of explicit political and social remarks? Beaumarchais, after all, represents a social order in which rank and its powers enter into and form the relations, above all the sexual relations, of these people, in ways which we are invited to deplore, just as we are invited to rejoice in, not merely be amused by, the Count's discomfiture.

It is no accident, relative to all that, that he is a count: this too, and perhaps more deeply, is social comment. But all that is equally true of what is given us by Da Ponte and Mozart; and in that sense, that too, perhaps more deeply still, can be seen as social comment. It is a mistake to oppose on the one hand the relations of social status and power between these characters, and on the other their personal and sexual relations: to a notable extent, the personal here implies and is built round the social.

That this can be so is after all a commonplace of European literature and drama; that it has been very little applied in writing about Mozart is perhaps just another indication of the fact that there has been very little serious opera criticism, and indeed very little belief that there could be such a thing. It is perhaps an effect of Peter Hall's experience of non-operatic drama that his marvellously well judged Glyndebourne production of *Figaro* succeeds in setting out concretely, clear-headedly and convincingly the complex nature of these relations.

Of course, it is one thing to show, as Mozart clearly does show, the inter-penetration of social power and sexual relations; another thing to offer a social critique; still another to offer a revolutionary critique. To what extent *Figaro* can be read as critique of any kind is a question I shall come back to at the end. First, we should look at what the opera does, above all what it shows us about the relations of the four chief characters. We should start with the Count, the formal holder of power: while it is the plans of the other characters that largely structure the drama, it is the Count's proj-ects, entirely, which occasion it. In Beaumarchais' play, it is said of the Count that he is a libertine from boredom, and jealous from vanity. Da Ponte only partly agrees, as we see in the brief recitative conversation between Susanna and the Countess at the beginning of Act II. Here, the Count is said to be like all modern husbands, unfaithful by design, and jealous from pride. This infidelity is different from that of Beaumarchais' Count, who is motivated above all by boredom, a boredom which is partly formed by his way of life, and is also, as he and the Countess individually tell us, the product of her tireless, but equally tiring, devotion to him. He is exhausted by her exceptional tenderness. Da Ponte's Count is also bored with the Countess, but he is specially labelled as a modern man who has a system: and it is appropriate that, having forsworn the *droit de seigneur*, his feudal rights, the Count should approach Susanna, as she tells us here, with that more modern device – a contract for money. What is clear here, in any case, is the contrast between what he could offer to Susanna, however much he wanted her, and what he used to offer the Countess; the Countess used to receive something called 'love', and no-one in Susanna's station can expect that from the Count. That certainly is a matter of class; and more so, in a way, in the opera than it is in Beaumarchais. For, in the play, that social thought has got attached to it a further and, as it were, compensating piece of cynicism, to the effect that the absence of love is after all only the absence of an illusion: as the Count says to Susanna in a marvellous epigram which Da Ponte does not match – love is only the fiction of the heart, it is pleasure which is its history.

Thus it is the lower classes who, as the objects of pleasure and not of love, can, in a way, represent reality. That idea is certainly, in that form, far removed from Mozart. Yet there is another version of that idea, a much less cynical version, which Mozart perhaps expresses, too. It can be heard most clearly in the contrast between the Countess's 'Porgi, amor' at the beginning of Act II and Susanna's 'Deh vieni, non tardar' in Act IV. The Countess's song expresses an abstract ideal; Susanna's expresses concrete present desire.

As for the Count, his frustration and his social contempt unite in his famous third-act outburst, 'Vedrò mentr'io sospiro', which is obsessed with the idea that the woman he desires should go to his servant: 'un vile oggetto', as he calls Figaro, a worthless object. Here, very plainly, sexual frustration and social affront combine in one unbearable assault on the self. The real cause of his anger, in fact, is the sheer and simple frustration of his will: it is power, rather than in the end desire, the baffling of which has led him to this extreme. In this, he is typically and totally the social master: it is not the content of his desires, but the mere fact of their existence, which constitutes for him their authority.

In this, Figaro stands in total contrast to the Count. The mere existence of obstacles to his projects does not elicit violence or frustration from him: it elicits cunning and action. He does not start out with the idea that the world will be responsive to his will. He starts out rather with the characteristic hope of the underprivileged, that, with luck, the will can find a hole or two in an unresponsive world. There is only one place at which real frustration, powerless bitterness, breaks out, in that same last-act jealousy aria: and it is all-important that it occurs, not because plans to his end are frustrated, but because the end itself seems to have vanished, when he thinks that he has lost Susanna, the sole purpose of all his resourcefulness. So long as his objective is there, Figaro is not to be put down by the fact that it takes a long way round to reach it: he would expect no less. His attitude is expressed quite wonderfully in the first-act aria 'Se vuol ballare', and in the delicate recitative which precedes it. When, in that, the orchestra has brushed in with the lightest of strokes the implications of Susanna's being the secret *attachée* of the Count, Figaro says firmly, 'non sarà', it shall not be. With the Count, those words would be a command; with Figaro, they are a decision to act.

'Se vuol ballare', memorably, comes back when, in Act II, after some complex conspiracy between Figaro, Susanna and a distinctly nervous Countess, Figaro reminds them, and above all the Countess, that it is his plans that are in hand. In Peter Hall's production, there is at this point a wonderful and revealing moment, when the Countess looks at Susanna and the departing Figaro suddenly aghast, realising that she has put herself into their power. It is an anticipation of something which the Countess herself will express in grander terms later, when in Act III, in the recitative to the nostalgic aria 'Dove sono', she expresses her shame and humiliation, not merely at the infidelity of her husband, but at the fact that that infidelity reduces her to seeking the help of her maid.

The Countess, though evidently a sympathetic character, which the Count barely is, nevertheless shares something with him which neither shares with the others: straightforwardly, rank, but as a result of rank, a certain unconquerable loneliness, which all the conspiracies and dressings-up and plots shared with valets or pages will not, even in her own mind, overcome. By comparison with the Countess, Susanna is a vastly freer figure. She could not marry the Count (and who but the Countess would want to?), but she has the power conferred by the fact that he wants her; her sex and her station together make her freer than anyone, freer indeed than Figaro himself, for she, Susanna, alone of the four, has some natural basis of relations with each of the others, unlike Figaro, who confronts the Count in rivalry, and the Countess with an unresolvable ambiguity about their relations. When, near the end of the last act, Figaro pretends to be making love to the Countess, it only makes sense because we know it is actually Susanna; what a real love scene between Figaro and the Countess would be like is quite unimaginable, while a real love scene between Susanna and the Count is something which we, and they, would know the nature of perfectly well.

The Countess is most alone; the Count, selfish though he is, relates in a way to Figaro and Susanna through power and rivalry and desire, but the Countess is left with not much except her memories, her fractured pride, and her mildly light-headed excitement with the unfocused sensuality of Cherubino. Or is she left also with hope? Here something turns on one's interpretation of the very end of the opera, above all of the deeply beautiful Andante chorus of forgiveness which breathtakingly holds the action utterly still before the very last moments of the bustling conclusion.

The critic Joseph Kerman has seen in this passage an anticipation of *The Magic Flute*, not only musically, but in the celebration of the superior love of a superior couple: 'The reconciliation of the Count and Countess,' he writes, 'is deep and true, the most beautiful thing in the opera.' He sees in them a noble couple capable at their best of heights of consciousness not available to the Papageno-Papagena level of Figaro and Susanna.

This view seems to me quite false to *Figaro*: it is an arch example, moreover, of a basic error in the appreciation of Mozart's operas, the idea that the relations of pairs of characters are parallel in different works, whereas in fact they are quite different and have to be understood, without prejudice, in each case. In that Andante, there is indeed a moment of calm, of attainment, and of complete understanding; but it does not, to me, imply that anything has basically changed for the Count and the Countess, or that even at this instant they are very close together: they are seeing more than usual, but they are doing so apart. The day's doings have probably left the Countess's loneliness very much where it was. Our straightforward reaction to the opera, that it is in Figaro and Susanna that some larger and more spontaneous humanity has triumphed, is surely right.

What then of the question of a social critique which I mentioned earlier? I hope the question, put in those terms, has by now lost some of its edge. If what is meant is a revolutionary critique, in the sense of one that shows the necessity, in order to cure human evils, of social or political action, then there is none of that in this work. But if what is meant by a social critique is a work which not merely displays human feelings and relations in a real social context, but shows those feelings as formed and distorted by that context, and shows also how rank can itself generate rage and loneliness, while lack of it can leave room for a greater openness, then *Figaro* is, among many other things, such a critique. It is not an inappropriate thing for one of the very greatest masterpieces of realistic art to be.

4

Don Giovanni as an Idea

Giovanni is Don Juan, but he does not have to bear the weight of all the significance which that mythical figure has come to express. Still less does Giovanni have to be pursued, as though by another Elvira, with every interpretation that has been given of Don Juanism as a psychological category: that it expresses latent homosexuality, for instance, or hatred of women, or a need for reassurance. Any of these may be true of the local womaniser, but he is not Giovanni, and these states of mind are not what *Don Giovanni* expresses.

Some later Don Juans, elaborated as they all are with a vast variety of metaphysical, social or psychological reflections, are closer relatives of Giovanni than others. Most remote are the negative, melancholic or merely frantic embodiments of the hero: fleeing from exhaustion and inner emptiness, in Lenau's representation, or, according to George Sand and Flaubert, engaged in a despairing hunt for a genuine encounter with another person. These, at any rate, are not Giovanni, who is as unambiguously and magnificently removed from despair and boredom as it is possible to be. At the climax of the opera, his words are in praise of women and wine, 'sostegno e gloria d'umanità' ('support and glory of mankind'), but his music encompasses a larger praise of life and humanity themselves.

This chapter is concerned only with Giovanni's closer relatives in the tradition. Moreover, it is interested in them only insofar as they seem to help in thinking about the opera. They are, of course, rarely independent of the opera. Later writers have not simply gone back to some archetype of Don Juan, or taken Mozart's opera merely as one previous embodiment of that character, but have in many cases been quite specially influenced by the opera. Indeed, nineteenth- and twentieth-century thoughts about Don

Juan have been dominated by Mozart's embodiment of him. This is not merely because the opera is by far the greatest work given to this theme. It is also because the opera is in various ways problematical, and because it raises in a challenging way the question of what the figure of Giovanni means. Hence, not only is the opera the historical starting-point of many modern thoughts on this subject, but some of those thoughts lead directly back to the problem of understanding the opera itself.

What are we to make of Giovanni? The opera is named after him, it is about him, it is he who holds together a set of scenes in other ways rather disconnected. He is in a deep way the life of the opera, yet the peculiarity is that such character as he has is not really as grand as that implies: he expresses more than he is. He seems to have no depth adequate to the work in which he plays the central role. He has, in a sense, a character – to a considerable extent a bad one. But we are not given any insight into what he really is, or what drives him on. We could not have been: it is not that there is something hidden in his soul. It is notable that he has no self-reflective aria – he never sings about himself, as Mozart's other central characters do. We have no sense of what he is like when he is by himself. He is presented always in action – the action, notoriously, of a seducer. The facts that the opera is of great and unsettling power, that a seducer is at the centre of it, and that the seducer is virtually characterless were brought together in one of the first and most important reflections on the wider significance of the work, Søren Kierkegaard's famous essay 'The Immediate Stages of the Erotic, or The Musical Erotic'. It was one of a set of essays that he published in 1843. They were not published under his own name; Kierkegaard appears under a pseudonym, and even under this he claims only to introduce two sets of papers, by authors 'A' and 'B'. The papers of 'A' present an aesthetic view of life, those of 'B' an ethical view. The disjunction between the two views – the 'Either/Or' of the book's title – is left before the reader. Through all this indirection, the account of *Don Giovanni* is of course Kierkegaard's; but the authorial evasions are important, and they encourage him, or permit him, to leave a central question unresolved.

It is important that Kierkegaard is writing about Mozart's opera, and not merely about the character of Don Juan in general. This is not simply because he regards Mozart's as the greatest embodiment of the character. Beyond that, he thinks that it is a basic truth about the character that this should be so, a truth which he tries to explain. Mozart's is the greatest embodiment because of a perfect match of medium and content: music is the most 'abstract' of the arts, and is therefore ideally suited to express the abstract principle of sensual desire itself. And since that principle is what, above all, music expresses, *Don Giovanni* will also be the greatest work of music, a consequence which, amid a good deal of ironical self-reproof about the absurdity of such judgments, Kierkegaard (or rather his surrogate 'A') more or less allows himself.

Giovanni is the spirit of sensuous desire. He is (in a characteristic phrase) 'flesh incarnate'. He represents the third, full and final stage of three forms of sensual interest, each of which has been represented by Mozart. The first, 'dreaming', is expressed in the tranquillity, the 'hushed melancholy', of Cherubino's feeling; the second, 'seeking', in Papageno's craving for discovery. Giovanni combines and goes beyond both of these attitudes, in full desire, in conquest. He is a seducer, yet it is not really he who seduces – rather 'he desires, and that desire acts seductively'. His is no particular or individual voice. It is the voice of all desire, and it speaks to all women: it is heard 'through the longing of all womanhood'. This is why Zerlina, the one woman whose attempted seduction is actually enacted for us, is rightly, and intentionally, an 'insignificant' character. Yet this conclusion itself raises a doubt. Zerlina has less to her than the other two women, and what in her responds to Giovanni – to his charm, his desire, and, as is made perfectly clear, his rank and money – is nothing very deeply hidden. Giovanni had been called upon on other occasions, surely, to exercise that more searching appeal of the stranger, which is brilliantly evoked in the novel by John Berger called *G.*, one of the latest re-enactments of the Don Juan theme – and also one in which the figure appears at his most anonymously impersonal:

> The stranger who desires you and convinces you it is truly you in all your particularity whom he desires, brings a message from all that you might be, to you as you actually are. Impatience to receive that message will be almost as strong as your sense of life itself. The desire to know oneself passes curiosity. But he must be a stranger, for the better you, that you actually are, know him, and likewise the better he knows you, the less he can reveal to you of your unknown but possible self. He must be a stranger.

In Zerlina it is no great distance to her unknown but possible self. It is a pity, one might feel, that Mozart did not enact for us the seduction of Donna Elvira – still more, of Donna Anna. According to E. T. A. Hoffmann's famous story, he did. Hoffmann represents Anna as actually seduced by Giovanni, and this fact as the ground of her response to him: 'She was not saved! when he rushed forth the deed was done. The fire of a superhuman sensuality, glowing from Hell, flowed through her innermost being and made her impotent to resist. Only he, only Don Juan, could arouse in her the lustful abandon with which she embraced him.' The idea that Anna succumbed to Giovanni had been anticipated by Goldoni; but the significance that Hoffmann gives to this idea, and the consequences of it for the character and power of Giovanni, are what make Hoffmann's tale more than an anecdotal extension of the traditional plot. Kierkegaard writes,

> But what is this force then by which Don Juan seduces? It is the power of desire, the energy of sensual desire. He desires in every woman the whole of womanhood, and therein lies the sensually idealizing power with which he at once embellishes and overcomes his prey. The reflex of his gigantic passion beautifies and develops its object, who flushes in enhanced beauty by its reflection. As the fire of ecstasy with its seductive splendor illumines even the stranger who happens to have some relation to him, so he transfigures in a far deeper sense every girl, since his relation to her is an essential one. Therefore all finite differences fade away before him in comparison with the main thing: being a woman. He rejuvenates the older woman into the beautiful middle-age of womanhood: he matures the child almost instantly: everything which is woman is his prey. On the other hand, we must by no means understand this as if his sensuality were blind; instinctively he knows very well how to discriminate, and above all, he idealizes.

The idea that Giovanni is in pursuit of the ideal was to have a good deal of later history; a similar representation of his aims was given by Théophile Gautier, who wrote, 'It is not vulgar debauchery that drives him on; he seeks the dream of his heart with the obstinacy of a Titan who fears neither thunder nor lightning.' It is one way of trying to express the true conviction that Giovanni, in his musical embodiment, means more than Giovanni, in his character as tireless seducer, could actually manage to be. But it does that in the wrong way. It betrays the opera by still resting firmly in the terms of masculine pursuit. The feminine appears still as an object, even though it is idealised – perhaps all the more so because it is idealised. That result cannot be adequate to Mozart's work. *Don Giovanni* is a story about a seducer, indeed about *the* seducer, and has him as hero, but no sensible person could think that it was a work that represented women as more passive than men, or as deriving the point of their existence only from being the object, especially the idealised object, of some essentially masculine principle. This is above all because it gives such a powerful sense of the individuality and the desires of the women in it.

The Romantic airlessness of 'the ideal' suffocates both the individuality and the desires of women. It has been suggested, in fact, that there is just one respect in which the seducer – the real seducer, who pursues women and not the ideal – is one who himself affirms the liberty of women: though he exploits or even destroys them, he does decline to imprison them in a possessive institution. Although he 'has' them or 'makes' them, he does not make them his. The catalogue, as Jean Massin has said, is the negation of the harem.

If we are to give Giovanni his full stature, the erotic principle with which he is identified needs to be taken in some sense which is more general, and at the same time more honestly realistic, than the pursuit of the 'feminine ideal'. Kierkegaard himself seems to realise this, for later in his essay Giovanni is associated more generally with 'exuberant joy of life'. All the other characters have, compared with him, only a 'derived existence': he is 'the life principle within them'. It is the idea of Giovanni as a principle of vitality which explains, for instance, Leporello's attachment to him: he is absorbed, involved, swept up by him. Some idea of Giovanni as embodying the 'life force' is of course also what Shaw offers in *Man and Superman*; but in that enactment, seductive power and attractiveness have been replaced by a boundless loquacity, and the life force is extinguished among disquisitions on Darwinism and mournfully parochial paradoxes about the predatoriness of women. The preface of the play is only too appropriately subscribed, 'Woking, 1903'.

Now that Giovanni has come to be identified with something as general as the living principle of all the characters, the centre of their vitality, a difficulty arises; and since that identification has something right about it, and expresses convincingly Giovanni's musical relation to the rest of the opera, it is a real difficulty, which everyone has to face. Has Giovanni any longer a relation to either the social order or an order of divine judgment? When he was just a finite and particular kind of sexual brigand, there was no mystery in the idea that he should be hunted, prosecuted or damned; but when he has taken on this larger and more abstract significance, is there anything left to the idea of an order against which he is to be judged? In particular, what do we make of his end?

There is no clear or adequate answer to this question in Kierkegaard's own essay. He indeed notably plays down Giovanni's nastiness – he denies that he is really a schemer or even a deceiver, just because he is always energy in action, unselfconsciousness. When Giovanni becomes as idealised as this – so that he seems an innocent, the *Erdgeist*, a male, active, and unvictimised Lulu – the question of the order that condemns him becomes a very pressing one. Kierkegaard tell us, in effect, only that Giovanni is opposed to the spirit of Christianity, which is also (by a highly Hegelian identification) reflective spirit. This leaves us with an excessively blank fact, that Giovanni is breaking Christian laws and that is why he is punished. But that hardly says enough, even to Christians, if Giovanni indeed represents everyone's living principle. Kierkegaard himself perhaps escapes this criticism because he offers us in the essay only the view of 'A', the aesthetic view of life, and it is hardly surprising that he gestures only remotely towards the ethical. But the ethical will have to be got into closer relation to Giovanni than this, if Giovanni is everything that 'A' says that he is.

In distinguishing Mozart's Giovanni from an intriguer, Kierkegaard explicitly distinguishes him from Molière's Don Juan. That figure is driven particularly by the fear of boredom; the attempt to overcome satiation. Molière is mainly responsible for the idea of Don Juan as the amatory strategist, the hunter who is above all concerned with the tactics of the chase. It was a theme taken up later by Stendhal, who himself, however, finally pronounced in favour of Werther as opposed to Don Juan, the sentimental rather than the strategic. Stendhal's contrast, of course, relates simply to love – as something made, at any rate, if not felt. But the ruthless pursuer of love can come to represent, rather than one type of lover, one type of pursuer.

Simone de Beauvoir has said, 'If existentialism were solipsistic, the adventurer would be its perfect hero', and Giovanni is one type of the adventurer. He is a kind of nihilist, on this reading: one who indeed denies God and the fetishism of conventional moral approval and social rewards, and who lives through free action for its own sake. He represents 'the union of an original abundant vitality and reflective scepticism', but unlike the genuine and committed existentialist hero he has no sense of freedom as something all should share, and hence, like an adventurer in another style, Pizarro, he has contempt for other people. At the same time, he is dependent, dialectically, on social institutions which he rejects – wealth, and the liberty given by class.

Da Ponte constantly reminds us that Giovanni is a member of the nobility and that he deploys his rank and, as he himself very explicitly asserts, his money to get what he wants. He belongs of course to the equally noble world of Don Ottavio and Donna Anna, but we are left in no doubt what his contempt is for such a world, as a social order. When Masetto sees Zerlina being taken away from him by Giovanni and is prevented by Leporello from following, his outburst, 'Ho capito', combines the pains both of love and of social insult.

Formally there is a parallel here with the relations of Figaro and the Count, but there is also a basic difference. It is not only that Figaro is a complete person whereas Masetto is a more schematic and simpler character. Still less is it that Giovanni is the hero of his opera, while the Count is the villain of his – that oversimplifies our relations to both of them. Giovanni is not a hero we enter into, whereas, very strikingly, the point at which we are given the deepest and most sympathetic insight into the Count is in that aria ('Vedrò, mentr'io sospiro') in which he expresses the rage of baffled class power. The difference between the operas is that the Count and Figaro totally belong to the social world in which they are presented, and their motivations are naturally related to that world, whereas Giovanni is only making use of the social world in which he was born, and is basically a solitary figure who exploits but does not belong to his social surroundings. He is a brigand within his own country. He is at ease in being so, and Mozart is at ease in representing him so. While Giovanni is using his position, there is surely no ambivalence in it, or in the opera's attitude to it, such as Ernst Bloch suggested, who found in it the mark of 'a strangely ambiguous titanism' ('eines merkwürdig gesprenkelten Titanismus'), and asked, 'Is Don Giovanni, as Mozart shows him, a wolf or a human face under so many masks? Does he belong fully to the society of the *ancien régime*, as its most ruthless representative, or do we detect in him, in the erotic explosive rebellion, part of a return to nature?' Giovanni certainly lives off the land, but does so in an individual way that firmly refuses any such historical question. That he exploits others is identified by Simone de Beauvoir as a contradiction in the adventurer's situation – he both denies and affirms the need of his social background. But this is so, surely, only if he intends, or someone intends, his style of life to be an expression of freedom as something which everyone might try to follow. Giovanni himself entertains no such aspiration, nor does he reject it: he is not reflective in that style at all.

Nor in any other. It is this that marks him off from another great embodiment of reckless human energy with whom he has indeed been associated, Faust. A German author, Christian Dietrich Grabbe, produced in 1829 a play (*Don Juan und Faust*) which brought the two heroes together, a meeting which involves the following rather plodding exchange:

> *Don Juan*: Wozu übermenschlich
> Wenn du ein Mensch bleibst?
> *Faust*: Wozu Mensch
> Wenn du nach übermenschlichem nicht strebst?

> (*Don Juan*: What is the point of the superhuman
> If you remain man?
> *Faust*: What is the point of man
> If you do not strive for the superhuman?)

Such solemnities do not belong to the world of Giovanni. Even without them, Faust's undertaking, because it is essentially reflective, differs from Giovanni's. It is not merely that he is a scholar and an experimentalist, though that is true, and his attitude to Helen or Gretchen is of that kind. He loves or seduces as an experiment or an experience, in order to have done so, and that is the opposite of Giovanni, who simply says that he needs women 'more than I need the food that I eat or the air that I breathe'. More basically, Faust's whole bargain – what makes him the over-reacher he is – is reflective: it is a product of the calculation of the values of finite and infinite, and that is not a kind of enterprise known to Giovanni. As Camus remarked, Giovanni does not really believe in the after-life, unlike Faust, 'who believed enough in God to sell himself to the devil'.

But this leads us back to the questions about Giovanni's end; and whether it is, despite the opera's first title, *Il dissoluto punito*, a punishment. If the Commendatore is the veritable voice of Heaven, a Christian Sarastro so to speak, then Giovanni's defiance of him, the refusal of repentance in the face of a manifest miracle, is awesomely perverse. The celebration of Giovanni as Promethean hero, or – as by Musset and by Baudelaire, for example – as a figure of fascinating satanic evil, will then be in place. But Giovanni is not a satanic evil figure, and the extraordinary power his musical image expresses is not that of a tragic hero either. Camus is again to the point:

> Don Juan would find it natural that he should be punished. It is the rule of the game. And it is exactly a mark of his generosity, to have entirely accepted the rule of the game. But he knows that he is right, and that there can be no question of punishment. An inevitable end is not the same thing as a penalty.

If Giovanni's wilful defiance does not have a luciferian significance, then what he is defying cannot be God. The Commendatore in stone is on any showing an impressive figure: Shaw said that those trombones were 'a sound of dreadful joy to all musicians'. But his is not the voice of God. He is made of stone, and he does not come from Heaven (whatever he says about his diet), but from the churchyard where we first heard him. He is a terrible and unforeseen natural consequence of Giovanni's recklessness. He is indeed supernatural, but only in the sense of a realm of cause and effects which lie beyond the natural, not one that brings a new order of guilt and judgment. Giovanni's lofty refusal to repent when the statue demands that he should is not an ultimate offence to the cosmic order, but rather a splendidly attractive and grand refusal to be intimidated. If Giovanni's refusal were to be Faustian hubris or Promethean defiance, as some Romantic writers wanted, it would have to be something that he had come to after consideration. Mozart's tempi reveal it as convinced, but not as considered. The Commendatore's Andante gives Giovanni time to repent, but he does not give himself time, and could not do so. He is always in action; even when he is resting from one adventure, he is in flight for the next. His natural speed, throughout the opera, is that of 'Eh via buffone' (rather slower than 'Fin ch'han dal vino', a piece designed to show that even he can accelerate). That speed is not right for reflection; and no composer has ever found it the right speed for Faust. Shaw's Don Juan, by contrast, becalmed in that limitless lagoon of talk, loses his entire *raison d'être*.

The Commendatore does not need to be the voice of God; and the devils' chorus scarcely *could* be the sound of the Christian Inferno. The final sextet even refers to the place to which Don Giovanni has been removed, not by any Christian phrase, but in terms of the old creaking classical machinery of Proserpina and Pluto: Da Ponte attached no very great weight to that, no doubt, but it is quite right. Those old gods were themselves part of nature, and Giovanni's great virtue of courage, which he expressly boasts in his last moments, is displayed in a marvellous piece of consistency, of sufficiency, of bravado – a very proper and fine human reaction to something which, granted indeed his wicked life, is of the order of a vast and alarming natural consequence, rather than a transcendental judgment.

Curiously, each of Mozart's great Italian comedies has something unsatisfactory or problematic about its end. None of them perfectly solves the problem raised by its own depth – the problem of relating to the defining normality of comedy the intensity that the work has given to the irregular. Each promises a return to normality which it fails to define properly; each embodies some emotion which does not quite match the past or the future. In *Figaro*, there is the problem that at the end of the 'mad day', the Count and the Countess express reconciliation and forgiveness in music of such rapturous beauty that it can only be saying that all will be well for ever, when we know, from everything we have seen, that it cannot be for more than a week. In *Così fan tutte*, everybody is rattled back to their right partners in a manner which, granted what we have just been shown, can only be totally heartless. In *Don Giovanni*, the final sextet represents, very explicitly, a return to ordinary life. Should we take that to mean a return to the ordinary as against the supernatural, which has just done its work? Or a return to the decent with the end of the wicked?

There is certainly a return to the expected, after the intervention of the extraordinary. But that return does not define what has disappeared as simply wicked, indecent or unnecessary. In fact, the characters, with the exception of Zerlina and Masetto, scarcely do 'return to normal', but rather try to stick something together from what is left now that Giovanni has gone. Life without him will not merely be life with the wicked satisfactorily punished. Although his punishment is the subject of the closing words of the finale, and the moral of its 'antichissima canzon', Mozart has already shown us that life without Giovanni will be life that has lost a very powerful and single-minded embodiment of qualities which are indeed human. Because he was *just* those qualities, he himself lacked humanity – he was without love, compassion and fairness, to mention only a few of the things that he lacked. But the relation of what he had to what he lacked cannot be adequately expressed simply in terms of vice and virtue, dissoluteness and punishment, and that is something that Kierkegaard's interpretation half sees – sees, one might say, with half of him; but his essay leaves us, inadequately, still with the punishment as a blank require-ment of the Christian consciousness, besides contributing the ultimately sterile idea, favoured by some Romantics, that Giovanni's pursuit of women was more than it seemed because it was the pursuit of the ideal woman.

Contrary to that, other Romantics found his heroism in a displacement of ordinary virtue: face to face with the cosmic order, he defiantly, tragi-cally or even satanically rejects it. That account of him both overestimates the transcendental character of what he confronts, and underestimates the simply human, recognisable and invigorating quality of his attitude to that confrontation.

The sense of freedom that he expresses does not have all the metaphys-ical resonances that existentialist writers found in it, but it does have a significance which goes beyond an individual personal characteristic, and so does his recklessness. His single-minded determination to live at the fullest energy, at the extreme edge of desire, neglects consequences to himself as much as to others. Granted what makes life valuable to him, the ultimate consequences are irrelevant: cowardice, for him, would simply involve a misunderstanding of what was worth pursuing, just as consider-ateness (unless things happened to take him that way) would be a distrac-tion. He understands perfectly well that society exists – he can skilfully negotiate its obstacles. He understands that other people exist – how else could he so unfailingly find the 'unknown but possible self' of all those women? He has a perfectly clear idea of what might destroy him – his end is not just a mistake.

That end, however, and still more the essential closing bars of the opera that follow it, both affirm that there is no actual human life that could be lived as unconditionally as his. Those who survive Giovanni – not only the other characters, but, on each occasion that we have seen the opera, ourselves – are both more and less than he is: more, since the conditions *on* humanity, which we accept, are also the conditions *of* humanity; and less, since one thing vitality needs is to sustain the dream of being as free from conditions as he is.

BIBLIOGRAPHY

Baudelaire, Charles, 'La Fin de Don Juan', in *Œuvres posthumes* (Paris, 1887)

Beauvoir, Simone de, *Pour une morale de l'ambiguité* (Paris, 1961), trans. Bernard Frechtman, *The Ethics of Ambiguity* (New York, 1967), chapter 2

Berger, John, *G.* (London, 1972)

Bloch, Ernst, *Das Prinzip Hoffnung*, 3 vols (Berlin, 1953–6), part 5, section 49; 'Don Giovanni, alle Frauen und die Hochzeit'

Camus, Albert, *Le Mythe de Sisyphe* (Paris, 1942), 'Le Don-Juanisme'

Gautier, Théophile, *Histoire de l'art dramatique en France depuis vingt-cinq ans*, 6 vols (Paris, 1858–9), 'Italiens: *Don Giovanni*' (1845)

Hoffman, E. T. A., 'Don Juan', in *Sämtliche Werke*, vol. 1 (Munich and Leipzig, 1912)

Kierkegaard, Søren, *Either/Or*, 2 vols (1843; London, 1944), vol. 1, trans. David F. and Lillian Marvin Swenson. 'The Immediate Stages of the Erotic'; see also 'Diary of the Seducer'

Massin, Jean, *Don Juan, mythe littéraire et musical* (Paris, 1979) (texts, with commentary: Tirso, Molière, Hoffmann, Pushkin, Lenau, Baudelaire [in French], Da Ponte [in French and Italian])

Musset, Alfred de, 'La Matinée de Don Juan', *La France littéraire* (1883)

Shaw, George Bernard, *Man and Superman: A Comedy and a Philosophy* (London, 1903)

Shaw, George Bernard, 'Don Giovanni Explains' (1887), in *Short Stories, Scraps and Shavings* (London, 1934)

Shaw, George Bernard, *The Great Composers, Reviews and Bombardments*, ed. Louis Crompton (Berkeley and Los Angeles, 1978)

Stendhal (Henri Beyle), *De l'amour* (1822; Paris, 1959), chapter 59: 'Werther et Don Juan'

5

Passion and Cynicism

Remarks on *Così fan tutte*

To take *Così fan tutte* seriously is not, as people sometimes impatiently insist, to refuse to treat it as a comedy. On the contrary, it is to take it seriously as a comedy, something we are certainly prepared to do with other comedies, and with Mozart's other great Italian operas. Since one is dealing with an opera, that involves attending at once to the music and to the meaning of the action, and when one does that a problem certainly arises. I want to try to locate the problem, and explore one approach to dealing with it.

The problem arises from the undeniable presence of passion in the seductions of the second act. There is passion, though not very demandingly so, in Dorabella's sweet yielding to Guglielmo; it is overwhelmingly present in the very painful moments of the duet 'Fra gli amplessi', in which Fiordiligi tries to get away from Ferrando and is unanswerably prevented. Yet after these encounters which the music presents as emotionally real, and after the couples move on to a marriage which, although fake and contrived by the conspirators, nevertheless is heralded in music once more of real power, especially in the canon quartet 'E nel tuo, nel mio bicchiero' – after all that, the disguises are taken off, and everybody is hustled back to the person who is conventionally the right person and all ends in good cheer and the praise of reason. Something, it might be felt, is unsatisfactory in that ending.

Nearly every critic who has taken *Così* seriously has found something unsatisfactory about it. Beethoven disapproved of the plot, but then he disapproved of *Figaro* and *Don Giovanni* as well, and the point is therefore less interesting, since it is in comparison to them, rather than to *Fidelio*, that one first wants to look at *Così*. Wagner indeed did make that comparison, and thought that an unworthy subject had produced lesser music: 'How doubly dear and above all honour is Mozart to me,' he wrote, 'that it was *not* possible for him to invent music for . . . *Così fan tutte* like that of *Figaro*! How shamefully would it have desecrated music!'[1]

But that is not right; the upsetting feature of *Così* is not that this subject has elicited weak music, but that some of the music it has elicited is, so it seems, too strong, and puts a weight on the plot which its farcical artificiality cannot sustain. I do not believe that if Da Ponte's libretto had been set in a rattling bright superficial way by someone else it would ever have upset anyone. A *Così* by Rossini might have been trivial or boring, cynical indeed in an undemanding way, but certainly not upsetting. The problem is not merely that the libretto is cynical or silly or disagreeable about women. The problem is rather the emotional power which Mozart has vested in that artificial narrative structure, and cumulatively so through the second act until almost the end.

Since the great revival of interest in the work in the twentieth century, some critics have suggested that the problem was just the product of nineteenth-century moralistic limitations, and that if we take a sufficiently complex or ironical view of it, the work will be distanced enough to remove any discomfort. Richard Strauss referred to what he called 'the humorously pathetic and parodistically sentimental . . . delicate irony of *Così fan tutte*':[2] this wheezy accumulation of epithets only emphasises the central difficulty – that if the music which Mozart gives Fiordiligi's situation in the second act is a *parody,* then we have no reason to trust our emotional reactions to anything in Mozart's music at all. Edward Dent, again, grasped desperately at both horns of the dilemma, and said that the characters in *Così* were marionettes capable of an amazingly wide range of emotions[3] – a description which makes the work sound, if anything, like *Petrushka*.

Most recently, the doubts have come round again. In *Opera as Drama* Joseph Kerman refers to *Così* as 'Mozart's most problematic opera', and writes, 'Romantic critics considered [the story] outrageous, improbable, immoral, frivolous, unworthy of Mozart; the last two charges are true enough.' He argues that Da Ponte presented Mozart with a libretto unsuitable to his genius, so that an unhappy strain developed between the formal frivolities of the story and the feeling which Mozart could not hold back from his music.[4] Michael Tanner, in a radio talk, developed a particular version of such criticism, making the point that if we accept the invitation of the music to take seriously the feelings of Fiordiligi, the work reaches down to levels at which the behaviour of the men must be seen as both disagreeable and implausible.

In these criticisms we hear again the note of upset. The complaint is not merely that the work is in some formal or purely architectural terms awry, a technical failure; it is rather that the strain which develops between the text and the music generates something which is not just imperfect but unacceptable.

I agree with these critics that the later music is to be taken as seriously as it seems to demand. I also think that it is more than probable, historically, that Da Ponte produced one sort of thing and got from the hands of Mozart another, a very peculiar, sort of thing. It is also an upsetting thing. But it is upsetting not because it is a failure, or broken-backed, or the product of a misunderstanding, but because it succeeds in being upsetting, and because the irony it undoubtedly contains is not of the kind which the libretto, taken in itself, would seem to expect, but something much more bitter. It is not a perfect work (if one wants perfection in Mozart's comedies, it is to be found in *Figaro*), but it is a deep and unsettling masterpiece, which, like some other eighteenth-century works, plays disquietingly across the formalities of its structure. Above all, to see it as it is, we have to recognise that it is less like its two great companions, indeed less like anything else, than we tend to assume.

The Romantic critics were correct in a feeling that the work is in a sense cynical, but quite wrong about what that sense is. It may be that the libretto is, as Kerman says, 'firmly posited on the view that emotion is essentially trivial' (an opinion which he rather quaintly calls 'a legitimate comic exaggeration'), but, as Kerman also says, that is certainly not the view of Mozart, nor of *Così* taken as a whole. Its cynicism does not consist in saying that that is so. Nor does it really say that women in particular have light and silly emotions, as the title and motto formally suggest; if *Così* – taking it all the time as Mozart's *Così*, not just Da Ponte's – says anything special about women's feelings, it is that they are more serious than men's. What its cynicism consists in is rather the idea that emotions are indeed deep, indeed based in reality, but the world will go on as though they were not, and the social order, which looks to things other than those emotional forces, will win out. 'Will' win out, not 'must': the reach of the work is not wide enough, and the ambivalence of its end too great, to invite any universal suggestion. 'Look,' it rather says, 'this is very often how it is, that real forces of emotion and desire are met and acknowledged and carry the most serious conviction, yet the world rattles on as though it were not so; the conventional order makes its bleakly reasonable demands.'

If this is the major theme, then certain other things fall into place. For instance, there is no reason why the men should be very strongly individuated characters. It has been offered as a reproach to the work that they are not, and indeed the criticism has been extended to the sisters as well. In the case of the sisters, the criticism is just a mistake. They do start together, in Act I, in a public and social domain where there is not much to distinguish them, and where the stylistic variations in their conventional attitudes appropriately provide little leverage for character. But in Act II, as they move out into a world of genuine feeling, they are progressively separated, until Fiordiligi, who of course travels much further, reaches an entirely different place by herself.

The men's role, however, is quite different, and it is a misunderstanding to suppose, as many critics and productions do, that the basic units of the opera are the male-female couples. It is also a misunderstanding to think that we have to take each major character seriously as a person if we are to take the work seriously. This is not a work like *Figaro*, whose depth indeed consists in the depth of its individual characters. The men in *Così* represent in their disguise more a common sensual threat, their role as Albanians a light-heartedly exotic emblem of strong passions and pleasures. This aspect is wonderfully brought out by Mozart when we hear the men for the first time in Act II, in the luxurious serenade 'Secondate, aurette amiche' which they offer from a barge at the seashore. This has very much the same tone as a piece in the first act, the shimmering trio 'Soave sia il vento', which Don Alfonso and the two sisters sing after the men's supposed departure: already at that early moment – the earliest possible moment – we can hear something of the reserves of desire which are going to engulf these ladies' conventional commitments.

The impersonality of the men's sensual role extends beyond their joint efforts. It is almost equally impersonally that Ferrando plays his role as seducer of Fiordiligi: he is an embodiment of desire, a representative of a sort of force she has never had to face before. This element of abstraction from any concrete character gives a particular poignancy to that duet when Fiordiligi falls, which I have already mentioned, and of which Kerman rightly says that it is both the expressive and the dramatic centre of the work. Fiordiligi is pathetically planning to head for the wars, to join her proper man and escape these new feelings; the moment that she is interrupted by Ferrando's vocal entry on the line 'Ed intanto di dolore', we and she know that she is done for, and the effect is more unnerving because that pure tenor voice seems to arrive from nowhere.

There is a similarly seductive relation of those two voices in the canon before the supposed wedding celebration, when first Fiordiligi, then Ferrando and then Dorabella join in a toast which significantly says, 'E non resti più memoria del passato ai nostri cor' ('And let no memory of the past remain in our hearts'). The other man, Guglielmo, takes no part in this toast: his contribution to the quartet is confined to muttering curses against the women. There is a technical reason why he does not join in the canon, that it is too high for him; but in so building the quartet in the first place, Mozart surely found in the tenor voice, particularly after that earlier crucial duet, the right expression of the rapt involvement in which the women find themselves caught.

There is one place in which Guglielmo certainly branches out on a line of his own, and that, illuminatingly, is one of the weakest pieces in the opera: the diatribe against women, 'Donne mie, la fate a tanti'. The thinness of this aria is particularly striking when it is compared with its great predecessor in the same line of business, Figaro's aria 'Aprite un po' quegl'occhi', which it resembles in many respects, except that it lacks the musical and dramatic power, and the remarkable bitterness, of that extraordinary piece. Perhaps it was just a mistake for Mozart and Da Ponte to try to repeat an effect. I suspect, though, that the mistake goes deeper: that it was wrong to try to equip Guglielmo for a moment or two with the features of personal bitterness at all. That is not the sort of thing he and Ferrando are there to express. If we regard the work as an *éducation sentimentale* of the men, their growing up as individual persons to worldly wisdom with the help of Don Alfonso, then the piece is a failure; for one thing, at the end they seem not to have learnt much at all. But that is not the purpose, and there is no such failure. The men represent conventional suitors in one role, and the forces of desire in the other, and there is not all that much individual difference between them: Ferrando's demands, in his second role, go deeper, just because they are demands on Fiordiligi, who is more deeply affected.

There is not much bitterness represented *in* the characters of *Così* at all. Insofar as there is, it is largely concentrated in the few independent utterances of Don Alfonso, which sometimes have just the kind of disagreeable edge that Guglielmo's aria lacks; as in his serpentine contribution at the very beginning of the opera, 'È la fede delle femmine',[5] and in his motto piece just before the Act II finale. Alfonso is the proper repository of sourness inside *Così*, since he is the authorised representative of the conventional world.

But the real bitterness lies rather in what we see and feel happen to the characters; in the way in which these women meet these desires and demands, and in the case at least of one of them, discover a deep response to them; and are then briskly, indeed brutally, returned to a conventional arrangement which was grounded, as we were shown, in shallower sentiments. Nothing is denied of what has happened; that is what is sad in this comedy, that all that dimension of feeling exists, but the world will rumble on as though it did not. Perhaps it may even be hinted that it is better that the world and its arrangements turn their back on that kind and depth of feeling. If one feels that Mozart in this work agreed that it was better so, then one may be able to hear the ambivalent end of the second act as a convinced, if rather wry, celebration of a return from danger. If on the other hand one finds, as I do, that the end makes a rather stunned and hollow sound, one may feel that this work is more concerned to display the demands of the world against feeling than it is to justify them.

Notes

1. *Opera and Drama*, in *Wagner on Music and Drama*, selected by Albert Goldman and Evert Sprinchorn from translations by H. Ashton Ellis (London, 1970), p. 100.
2. Quoted in János Leibner, *Mozart on the Stage* (London, 1972), p. 219.
3. *Mozart's Operas*, 2nd edn (Oxford, 1991), p. 192.
4. *Opera as Drama* (New York, 1956), pp. 109ff.
5. The text carries a joke of its own: it is copied, all but one word, from a well-known aria text by Metastasio; see P. J. Smith, *The Tenth Muse* (London, 1971), p. 175.

6

Rather Red than Black

Verdi, *Don Carlos* and the Passion for Freedom

Don Carlos stands in a special relation to Verdi's social and political ideals – ideals which were themselves connected at more than one level with the aims of his art. It is those ideals I should like to say something about.

From the beginning Verdi's work was associated with liberal and nationalist causes. It is well known how in his first great success, *Nabucco*, the nostalgic chorus of Hebrew exiles, 'Va pensiero', became one of the great songs of the Italian aspiration to independence and unity. In the first decade of his work, other pieces, lines or situations in his operas were to be seized upon in Milan or Rome or Venice to the same effect, always to the composer's satisfaction and often as part of his purpose. At his funeral nearly sixty years later, the vast crowd spontaneously broke into it.

In that decade of the 1840s Italy was divided, and for the most part ruled by foreign powers; and the aim of removing foreign power came to embrace, equally, the cause of Italian unity – Mazzini insisted, an independent Italy had to be a unified Italy. Verdi himself was single-mindedly dedicated to this idea; and when later, in 1859, Lombardy was enabled to join a free Piedmont, but Venice remained under Austria, Verdi was totally disgusted.

It was this cause of Italian unity that the public found expressed in several of the operas of the 1840s. In *I Lombardi alla prima crociata*, at its first performance in 1843, the Lombards were readily taken as the Italians, the Saracens as the Austrians, and when in the last act the Lombards were incited to battle with the words 'The Holy Land will be ours today!' there were enthusiastic cries. Three years later, the line in *Attila*, uttered by a Roman general, 'You can have the universe, let Italy remain with me', set by

Verdi in a compelling manner, aroused shouts of 'A noi! L'Italia a noi!' and
became instantly famous.

The nationalist appeal was not unintentional, though certainly it was
not Verdi's aim to write patriotic operas entirely for their own sake; these
were the years of many operas, some pretty crude, and of much drudgery,
the time he was to call the years in the galleys, and a lot later his second
wife Giuseppina was to imply that his overwhelming aim at this time
had been to make money. But that aim did not prevent these works
progressively strengthening his art; nor from revealing, if only in choice
of subject or emphasis, his nationalist sympathies.

But there was one opera which Verdi wrote specifically to a nationalist
theme, encouraged it seems by a letter from the poet Giuseppe Giusti, who
reproved him for his choice of the foreign topic of *Macbeth*, and urged him
to accompany 'the high and solemn sorrow [of the Italian people] with
your noble harmonies'. The work that issued from this was *La battaglia di
Legnano*, which was first put on in Rome on 27 January 1849, at the
moment of high republican and nationalist enthusiasm. The Pope had fled
Rome, Garibaldi and Mazzini had both arrived in the city, and it looked as
though the Papal States were about to be declared a republic. The moment,
like many other moments of hope for Italian liberty, passed, but it was a
fine moment, in particular for *La battaglia di Legnano*. The work was
received with wild enthusiasm, the whole of the fourth act was encored at
each performance, and on the first night, when at the end of Act III the
hero with a cry of 'Viva Italia!' leaps off a balcony to rejoin his regiment,
a soldier in the fourth tier threw onto the stage his coat, his sword and all
the chairs in the box. This was an opera to which Verdi in later years felt
some attachment; at least he felt that he had produced a substantial and
independent work of art.

It was not until ten years after this, at the first production of *Un ballo in
maschera* in 1859, that the cry of 'Viva Verdi' first took on the particular
nationalist significance which it was famously to bear, by which the letters
VERDI were taken as an acronym of Vittorio Emanuele, Re d'Italia. By that
happy idea, Verdi's name became almost literally synonymous with that of
the figurehead of Italian unity. But it was in the first ten years that his work
had conspicuously earned him that association. It had earned it not just by
choice of subject and a well-judged emphasis on the appropriate situations. It owed it also, and more deeply, to his style, a style which was direct
in its effect and popular in its origins.

Verdi had throughout his life what may rather vaguely be called nation-alist opinions about musical style, and in his later years was rather given to saying that Wagner was all right for Germans to follow but not Italians; that there should be not chamber music societies in Italy but more vocal groups; and so forth. It was in the vocal tradition that he identified the Italian musical genius, a tradition he saw going back far beyond the origins of Romantic opera, notably to Palestrina. He saw himself as belonging to and having developed that tradition for his own purposes of dramatic expression. He did not see himself as having invented anything like a new national language, in the sense in which the novelist Manzoni – the man whom Verdi venerated more than any other – had founded a new national language of literary expression in *I promessi sposi*. Rossini, Bellini, Donizetti had of course already been national figures, nationally admired. Yet the enormous vigour and energy of Verdi's music represent the tapping of a popular tradition in a way different from anything found in his predecessors. Particularly in these earlier works it showed itself in his use of that manifestly popular form, the chorus. Already in 1844 Verdi was known to the Milanese as 'the father of the chorus'; and Julian Budden has written, 'Patriotic choruses, rousing or nostalgic, figure in most Verdi operas from *Nabucco to La battaglia di Legnano* . . . Naive though they are, Verdi was never ashamed of these patriotic choruses . . . they were written with the greatest sincerity of purpose . . . For him the nationalism of the *Risorgimento* was the gateway to a wider and grander conception of humanity.'

What then were the conceptions that underlay Verdi's nationalism? In trying to see something of the view of life and of politics which drew him to that cause, one may also see something of the continuities between the early patriotic manifestations and the passion for liberty which plays such an important role in *Don Carlos*. Nationalism in Italy was, as elsewhere, deeply connected with the spirit of Romanticism; peculiar features of Italy made that connection particularly simple and direct, the impulse of Romanticism in Italy expressing itself politically as a liberal form of nationalism – there was not much room in the Italian scene for reac-tionary, medievalising, or paternalist nationalism which elsewhere could also grow from Romantic roots. Verdi was this kind of liberal Romantic, dedicated to ideals of individual as well as of national liberty. He was a Romantic also in his views on the national spirit in art, which I have mentioned; and a Romantic, also, in what he thought about the relations between art, individual expression and tradition – on these matters Verdi's outlook was in fact, strange though it may seem, almost exactly the same as that endorsed by Wagner in *Die Meistersinger*.

In a more superficial sense of 'Romantic', however, Verdi's nationalism was not Romantic, and it is significant that the political figure of the Risorgimento whom he devotedly admired was not the solitary and visionary Mazzini nor the adventurer Garibaldi ('ingenuous' Giuseppina called *him* in 1864) but the cautious diplomat Cavour, of whom it has been said that he had middle-class aims and an aristocratic style. Verdi was devoted to Cavour, and it was Cavour who personally persuaded Verdi into the highly improbable undertaking of becoming a Deputy in the first Parliament of a united Italy in Turin.

He was elected in February 1861 after a rather painful misunderstanding with one Minghelli-Vaini, an alternative candidate, which elicited from Verdi the most touchy declarations to the effect that he would not lift a finger to get himself elected – 'the word "intrigue" does not exist in my dictionary,' he said. Cavour died in June of that same year, which as well as a blow to Italy was a blow to Verdi personally, and more or less marked the end of his hardly existent political career. He stayed away from the Chamber for more than two years, and then attended very rarely: his offers to resign were resisted. As he wrote to the librettist Piave, 'If anyone needed to write about my career as a member of Parliament, he would only have to print in the centre of a beautiful piece of paper, "The 450 are really only 449, for Verdi as a Deputy doesn't exist."'

'I am a liberal to the utmost degree, without being a Red' – this he wrote in a set of private notes about his grievances against the tiresome citizens of Busseto. 'I respect the liberty of others, and I demand respect for my own. The town is anything but Liberal. It makes a show of being so, perhaps out of fear, but is of clerical tendencies.' Two elements here are close to the heart of Verdi's outlook: on the one hand, a very strong sense of personal independence and integrity, and on the other, anti-clericalism. His anti-clericalism, which is expressed in *Don Carlos* as in no other of his works, was notably strong. He seems in any case quite possibly to have been an atheist (or agnostic, given his Christian burial). 'You're all mad,' he would say to Giuseppina when she displayed religious enthusiasm – but beyond that a specific distrust of the Church, as with many liberal Italians, then and now, played an integral part in his outlook. 'I cannot reconcile', he wrote in 1870, 'Parliament and the College of Cardinals, freedom of the press and Inquisition, the Civil Code and the Syllabus ... Perhaps tomorrow there will come a shrewd and clever Pope, such as Rome has had so many times before, and he will ruin us. *Pope* and *King of Italy* – I can't see them together even on the paper of this letter.'

Although he said, as we have seen, that he was no Red, he could go so far as to say that faced with a choice between Red and Black – that is to say, between the Left and the Catholic Right – he would rather have Red than Black. It was not the colour of the man that he worried about, but his worth, he used to say – not the *colore*, but the *valore*. 'Colours don't frighten me, but I do believe, and always will believe, that it is men of talent and good sense who keep the world going.' 'It is a strange thing,' he reflected in 1877, 'that in these times of freedom, no-one feels any more free, nor has the courage to tell the truth.' Courage, pride, independence, straightforwardness and good sense he admired; vanity, prejudice and intrigue he despised. It was indeed that mixture of middle-class and aristocratic virtues that he admired in Cavour.

Don Carlos is unique among Verdi's works in the weight and complexity of its political content, and in the way in which that content is related to personal character. The Council Chamber scene in *Simone Boccanegra* is of similar power – a late addition to that work, belonging to the years of Verdi's most mature works; but what that great appeal against faction does is to raise to a new level of dignity, and relate more interestingly to individual character, that same ideal of national unity that was voiced in the earliest works. In *Don Carlos* there is something quite different: a clash between persons which is also a clash of political outlooks which can each be taken seriously. Moreover, there is also a clash within a person, King Philip, which is a product of the *use* he has to make of his political power, and of the *limitations* on that power.

The clash between outlooks is centred, of course, in the duet between Posa and the King in Act II of the five-act version – that is, where Posa pleads for liberty in Flanders. This confrontation, central also to Schiller's play, was introduced into the libretto at Verdi's own suggestion. And the hard work on composing it made him, he said, 'spit blood'. There is no doubt who in this duet represents the right side, so to speak; Posa's music not only here but elsewhere, all the way in fact to his dying cry, offers once more a high expression of those aspirations that go back to *Nabucco*. That fact, together with the special weight which is conferred in all Verdi's work by the baritone voice, inevitably makes Posa seem the most serious embodiment of the noble cause, more serious in fact than Don Carlos, whose conversion to the cause of Flanders runs a certain risk by comparison of seeming like a hysterical flight from hopeless love to the Foreign Legion. At best, in his political undertakings Carlos looks like Garibaldi as compared with Posa's Cavour, Verdi's hero.

But while Posa is on the side of right, it is striking what weight Verdi's treatment gives the outlook of Philip, his arguments for tyranny and the pessimistic knowledge which he claims of the human heart. There is nothing unique in Verdi's finding power and deep interest in a character who is dark and in terms of the drama unsympathetic: Iago came later than King Philip, but many years before, equally, there was Lady Macbeth. What is unique is the weight lent to an outlook which supports tyranny and stands directly against the ideals of liberty and enlightenment. That outlook, moreover, we see – or rather, musically hear – is of a piece with the personal despair which Philip expresses in his aria in Act IV; and that solo, which shows the hopelessness in his own life and affections, leads in turn into the interview with the Grand Inquisitor – a conjunction of scenes which as an expression of the limitations of the King's power, both internally and externally, is quite extraordinary. The Church, in the person of the Inquisitor, acts as an independent force; we are shown the power it has, and over Philip, when we are shown the Inquisitor's ability to control events which Philip cannot control. Philip's dark outlook, as empty as his personal life, is yet not as wholly black as the power of the Church, which is the basis of his power and hence its limitations.

Don Carlos gives a strong sense of a political and social world within which the principal characters move: this is particularly so when the opening scene is restored which places Elisabeth's marriage in the context of the sufferings of war. This sense of a surrounding world shaped by social forces is no new thing for Verdi: on the contrary, it is an absolutely general feature of his operas that one should feel that the central action, however melodramatic or extravagant, is occurring in a surrounding world of crowds, society, other people pursuing their own lives. It is one of the conspicuous differences between his work and Wagner's.

However, *Don Carlos* also displays something else less usual in Verdi: Philip, its central figure – central in the sense that everything revolves round him – reveals a kind of complexity of character and motivation, especially in relation to political realities, which reaches beyond the familiar situation of a person in conflict between two affections or courses of action, to a deeper level. His outlook is darkened, not just by simple misery or simple wickedness or simple despair, but by a cloud of hopelessness which spreads over his personal and his public concerns, so that he no longer understands them properly. This has an implication for his political outlook itself. And part of the poignancy of his relations with Posa comes from the fact that he has no adequate way of fitting together his liking and admiration for that man with the view of the world which goes with his own power and its basis. That kind of darkness is new, perhaps unique, in Verdi. Ambiguity, ambivalence and a character's lack of identification with what he is doing – these are not in general the materials of his dramatic art: that is another conspicuous difference between him and Wagner.

In an age overwhelmingly impressed by the claims of those elements in drama, this absence raises the question of how it is we can take Verdi seriously (those elements are hardly absent, for instance, from his master Shakespeare). For some works, some passages, the truth is that we can't: as with much other Italian opera, as also with a lot of old films, there has to be an element of what you might call 'camp' in our enjoyment of them, meaning that the enjoyment depends on not accepting the ends that the works themselves had, but, rather, ironically and condescendingly distancing those ends.

But with many of Verdi's works, including of course *Don Carlos*, it is beyond question that we can take them fully seriously, and that our involvement in them is unreserved. To try to enquire exactly how and when that can be so would take us too far; for now, we can just notice that when it *is* so, Verdi's expression of his characters' typically energetic and direct reaction to the circumstances, and above all Verdi's unusual expression of that, creates in the audience a feeling of liberation, a sense of committed and energetic individual action, which is deeply invigorating. This experience is the basic, central, response to Verdi's art; almost all other responses to it grow out from, are sophistications of, that one.

In reflecting on that response, we can perhaps see at a rather different level now why it was not just because of patriotic choruses or his own expressed opinions that Verdi was rightly sensed to be the musical dramatist of liberalism. His characters do not need to be expressing sentiments in favour of liberty and honesty: the very method of expression itself conveys the importance and value of resolute individual action, untrammelled response to circumstance, and integrity of character.

Verdi's work sometimes directly expresses the values he believed in; in its entire conception it embodies them.

It is these same features that contribute to that sense of life which his works, even in their most ingenuous content, convey. Verdi possessed this himself. It was touched on by Boito, Verdi's collaborator of his last years, in a letter he wrote three months after Verdi's death. Boito was a highly sophisticated man, more sophisticated than Verdi; when he was young he was sceptical of Verdi's work but became utterly devoted to him. I will end with some words from that letter: they go straight to the source of Verdi's strength:

> In the course of my life I have lost those I idolized . . . But never have I experienced such a feeling of hatred against death, of contempt for that mysterious, blind, stupid, triumphant and craven power. It needed the death of this octogenarian to arouse these feelings in me.
>
> He too, hated it, for he was the most powerful expression of life that it is possible to imagine. He hated it as he hated laziness, enigmas and doubt.
>
> (Frank Walker, *The Man Verdi* (London, 1962) p. 509)

7

Tristan and Time

The action of *Tristan und Isolde* does not lie in external events. In this work Wagner carried to the extreme the process that was always basic to his dramatic method, of internalising the action and making the music expressive of inner states and of the deepest movements of the mind. In order to do that, he not only drastically pruned the traditional legend of persons and happenings, but also, in a way that was totally original, adjusted the time of his drama – both in its tempo, and in the order in which it reveals its images and explanations – to the flow of its characters' emotions, motivations and self-understanding.

The external events of *Tristan* are concentrated into very short episodes which occur at or near the end of each act. This helps to set up a parallelism of structure between the acts, which extends to other features as well. Thus each act starts with music off-stage, which provides the basis for at least the opening musical development. The dramatic content of that music, moreover, establishes in each act a different relation to time. In the first act, it is to the future; in the second, to the present; while in the third act it is, in an ultimate and revelatory way, to the past. These temporal references powerfully shape each act, and also combine to give the work, for all its apparent slowness and its emotional density, its sense of irresistible movement.

The sailor's song at the beginning, drifting down from high on the mast, looks forward,

Frisch weht der Wind
der Heimat zu

(Fresh blows the breeze towards the home country)

and the progress of the act is marked by reminders that the ship is rapidly approaching Cornwall, an arrival which Isolde knows she cannot endure. The constant sense of that approaching future helps to hold the act together. Within this forward-looking structure, Isolde turns to the past. In the long passage usually called 'Isolde's narration' she tells how she had earlier spared Tristan's life, and how he had then come back to lead her off to marry someone else. This retrospection is so placed within the forward movement of the act that it cannot possibly give the sense of being an expository device: it is not merely (as it is in some of Verdi's operas, for instance) that some things have to be told rather than shown because there is no time to show everything. These events are expressed in this way because Isolde carries them within her, and we have the sense, not so much of being told about the past, as of looking within her, and seeing, above all, one image:

Von seinem Lager
blickt' er her –
nicht auf das Schwert,
nicht auf die Hand –
er sah mir in die Augen.

(From his bed he looked up – not at the Sword, not at the hand – he looked into my eyes.)

Tristan's feelings, by contrast, are understood here as they appear to others, and insofar as he expresses them himself, they are expressed negatively: in gloom, appeals to convention, excuses, silence and, finally, a willingness that she should kill him. He will consciously recover his past in passages in the following acts, most poignantly during the third act monologue.

The hunting horns with which the second act begins relate to the present and to what, they pretend, is happening elsewhere. They already tell us, and Brangäne's repeated warnings remind us, of something that Tristan's and Isolde's music denies, that they are surrounded at that very time by an actual world of social and personal relations, some true, some dishonest – to which Mark's long recriminations give expression. Those recriminations, characteristically of Wagner, include a complex psychological account of the relations of the three people but, by that very fact, they are barely relevant to the state that Tristan and Isolde have reached.

That state is one in which they seek to escape altogether from the present, the passage of time and the world.

> O sink hernieder
> Nacht der Liebe
>
> (O descend, night of love)

the love duet begins,

> gib Vergessen
> dass ich lebe, . . .
> lose von
> der Welt mich los
>
> (give forgetfulness that I may live, . . . let me leave the world behind)

and before that there has already emerged a dominant image of the whole work, the contrast of healing dark with deceitful and damaging light, and with it the idea that the final consummation of love must lie in night, forgetfulness, death, and escape from the illusions and pain which are associated with day. Just as the signal for the lovers' meeting is the extinguishing of the light, so Tristan says that the love potion, when he drank it believing that it would lead to death, unlocked for him

> das Wunderreich der Nacht
>
> (the magical realm of night)

That dream of merging into non-existence, of never waking again, of dying while living for love, seeks to break out of time and individuality; but we are not allowed to forget, or only for a short while in the second act, that it is expressed in the midst of a real present and of real people elsewhere, a reality which it denies but which, with the most physically assaulting of all discords, finally breaks into it.

In a famous letter to Liszt, Wagner wrote of his plans for *Tristan*, 'Since I have never enjoyed in life the true happiness of love, I shall raise a monument to this most beautiful of all dreams, in which from beginning to end this love shall for once be completely fulfilled.' But, whatever dream is fulfilled in *Tristan*, it surely is not that of the true happiness of love – in any terms, at least, on which that could be enjoyed in life, or one could even dream that it might be enjoyed in life. *Tristan* is indeed true to another thought that Wagner expressed (to Cosima, in relation to Siegfried's fear): 'The kiss of love is the first intimation of death: the cessation of individuality'. But neither Tristan's love, nor his death, can attain its proper significance just by his passing from the one to the other – by his falling on Melot's sword and dying then and there. He has to pass through knowledge, and that is the subject of the last act.

In the third act, we have Tristan without Isolde, and it becomes finally his drama. In the first act, she was more conscious and active than he, but here he is the protagonist, he creates the inner conditions of his death, and she can only bless their love and follow him. Tristan's great monologue, the true climax of the whole work, falls into two spans, the first ending in the delusion that Isolde has arrived, and the second in the reality of that arrival. When he regains consciousness at the beginning of the act, he has returned from the borders of death, from being indeed and for a long time

> im weiten Reich
> der Weltennacht

> (in the broad realm of the world's night)

and he is forced back to the hated world of light, its destructive power now concentrated in the glare of the sun. At the beginning of the monologue, again at its quiet centre, and throughout central to its musical structure is the sad tune of the shepherd's pipe, 'die alte Weise' ('the old song'), and it is this that in the second part of the monologue leads Tristan back to the past. He goes deep into memory; to his orphaned childhood, to his earliest and recurrent longings, to his healing by Isolde, and to the potion. At the climax, he becomes fully conscious of their passion and its suffering, and takes full responsibility for that suffering:

> Den furchtbaren Trank! . . .
> ich selbst – ich selbst,
> ich hab' ihn gebraüt.

> (That terrible drink! . . . I myself – I myself, I brewed it!)

When Tristan dies, it is not merely by the ebbing of individuality into darkness, as at the beginning of the act he had wished, but in a state of ecstasy which has been reached by his acknowledging the roots of his suffering in himself.

Critics have tried in more than one way to describe the sense of release, enlightenment, indeed of achievement, that is finally brought about by the end of *Tristan*, some (notably Nietzsche) seeing it as tragedy, others as a symbol of mystical experience. Certainly it reaches further and deeper than a particular Romantic association of death, sexual love and the loss of identity, central as that undoubtedly is to the imagery of the love music. But in whatever direction one may further explore these meanings, it is certain that the significance of Tristan's last transformation lies in the fact that it is precipitated through recollection, and by a return to his past. That is the final achievement in this work of Wagner's mastery of the perspectives of time.

8

The Elusiveness of Pessimism

Responding to the *Ring*

The *Ring*, as a text, grew from *Siegfrieds Tod*, the single opera of which Wagner wrote the poem (and made a few musical sketches) before he conceived the cycle as a whole. In becoming *Götterdämmerung*, that work was changed in several ways, above all in its ending. *Siegfrieds Tod* closes, as *Götterdämmerung* does, with Brünnhilde riding into Siegfried's pyre, the flooding of the Rhine, and the return of the ring to the Rhinemaidens; but the gods are not overcome, Wotan rules for ever, and Brünnhilde takes Siegfried with her to Valhalla. The change from this triumphalist conception to the work as we have it, with the ending that is announced in its title, is of course deeply connected with much else that has happened in the cycle, and this is borne out by the strong sense one has that in ending like this, the *Ring* ends rightly.

   This is all the more striking because at a mechanical level of the plot there is a problem, which Wagner's friend Röckel pointed out as soon as he saw the privately published version of the *Ring* poem in 1853: 'Why, seeing that the gold is returned to the Rhine, is it necessary for the gods to perish?' He had a point, since we are told in *Götterdämmerung* itself (in the scene usually called 'Waltraute's narration') of Wotan's having said that if Brünnhilde gave back the ring to the Rhinemaidens, the curse would be lifted from the gods and from the world. In his reply to Röckel, Wagner admitted that the destruction was not in those terms absolutely necessary – a clever lawyer, as he put it, could argue that the conditions had been fulfilled – but that what was important was that the audience would feel its inevitability. They would feel it, in fact, from early in the cycle, and when Loge in the closing moments of *Rheingold* says, 'Ihrem Ende eilen sie zu, die so stark im Bestehen sich wähnen' ('They are hurrying to their end, who think themselves so strong and enduring'), 'in that moment he only gives expression to our own thought; for anyone who has followed *Rheingold* sympathetically, not cudgelling his brains over it but letting the events work on his feelings, must agree with Loge entirely'. We, surely, must agree with Wagner entirely: not so much because he was the creator of it all, but because what he said is clearly right.

The end of the gods has in fact been announced earlier in *Rheingold*. In her dark and impressive intervention, Erda tells Wotan to yield the ring to the giants and escape the curse on it. That sounds like a suggestion of how he might avoid destruction. But, having reminded him that she knows everything, she says, 'Höre! ... Alles was ist, endet! Ein düstrer Tag dämmert den Göttern' ('Listen ... All that exists is ending. A dark day dawns for the gods'), and though she follows this with a last warning, 'I advise you to avoid the ring', she leaves the prediction behind her, as she sinks into the ground, in a form that may be obscure but is certainly unconditional. She has not announced a bargain or a recipe.

Götterdämmerung is not an 'if only ...' story. In particular, it does not invite us to think how things would have been if only the Rhinemaidens had, somehow or other, got back the ring. We are shown that this is not the point by the incident at the beginning of the third act in which Siegfried himself encounters the Rhinemaidens: a scene more important than its rather arch and hearty manner may encourage one to think. At one moment, Siegfried actually offers to give them the ring, but they will not let him do so until they have told him about its powers and the curse upon it. It will not mean anything for him to give it back, unless he knows what he is doing. But this means that it is not just an ironical accident, but a certainty, that he will not properly give it back, since it is Siegfried's defining characteristic in this tale that he never knows what he is doing. In asking what sort of story *Götterdämmerung* is, we should recognise that Siegfried's lack of understanding is a crucial part of it.

He is the least self-aware, in every sense of the word the least knowing, of Wagner's heroes. He does not know much about anything, least of all about himself, and a lot of what he does know he forgets for most of the action, under the influence of Hagen's drug. (The music, of course, forgets those things as well. In a preliminary sketch, Wagner included in the scene with the Rhinemaidens a phrase associated with Brünnhilde, which he later removed.) Siegfried forgets, indeed, more than he strictly should. He cannot remember, it seems, that in his disguise as Gunther he took the ring from Brünnhilde, although he can remember other details of what he did then, for instance that they slept separated by the sword. This curious blank makes the action in the middle of the second act, when Brünnhilde arrives at the Gibichungs' hall, notoriously hard to follow. But the blank is in fact wonderfully appropriate to him. Violence of that kind cannot be part of the vacuously innocent self-image that he brings to Gutrune.

Although, in his dying moments, the memories of his love for Brünnhilde are restored to him, they do not bring with them any greater understanding, but only a return to a blissful past. In this, and in his relation to these magic drinks, he is quite unlike Tristan, who in his great monologue in the last act comes to see how everything that happened flowed from himself – that he himself, as he says, brewed the love potion. To Siegfried, on the other hand, the machinery of spells remains quite external, and represents nothing in his motivations or his wishes. It only summarises some of his qualities, in particular his limitless – one might almost say clinical – guilelessness and his destructively simple view of what it is to achieve anything.

His encounter with Brünnhilde did teach him something: fear. 'The kiss of love is the first intimation of death, the cessation of individuality,' Wagner said to Cosima; 'that is why Siegfried is so frightened.' This gave him a new experience, but nothing to carry forward from it except a blissful memory; and when he reasserts his individuality as a hero and returns to the world of action, there is no project for him except action itself. 'Zu neuen Taten!' ('New deeds!'), is the first thing that Brünnhilde says to him in *Götterdämmerung*, and, granted that he is to resume the only life he is able to live, there is nothing else for her to say about it. Just because he does not learn, Siegfried is significantly different, also, from Parsifal. He, though more famously a fool, gains something more from his first sexual encounter. Because it arouses in him not fear but guilt, he acquires understanding from it and comes back a changed person, one who can now be a king.

The only person in the world of *Götterdämmerung* who is or could be a king (in a more vigorously political manner than Parsifal) is, of course, absent from the action. But we are ceaselessly reminded of Wotan's existence and of his previous struggles, from the Norns' fragmentary survey of the world at the beginning, to Brünnhilde's closing words addressed to him, through Waltraute's and Alberich's interventions, and by such details as the fact that in the oath trio that ends the second act, Gunther and Brünnhilde swear to Wotan, while Hagen swears to Alberich, Wotan's dark counterpart. Wotan, unlike Siegfried, does understand – too much, and too soon. In that same letter to Röckel in which he explained the inevitability of the ending, Wagner said that the spectator would also experience it in grasping the feelings of Wotan. Already in the second act of *Walküre* Wotan cries out that there is only one thing he now wants, 'das Ende, das Ende', the end of the gods, to which, he tells Erda in the third act of *Siegfried*, he is reconciled. He is reconciled to it, however, under a misconception. For at this point he believes that although he and the other gods will disappear, Siegfried in his innocence, and the awakened Brünnhilde, will do something called 'redeeming the world'. This is presented as an entirely positive conception, its announcement accompanied by the first occurrence of a triumphant motive that will become associated with Siegfried and Brünnhilde's love.

Do Siegfried and Brünnhilde, by their love or their deaths, finally redeem the world, if not in the positive way that Wotan at that point seemed to expect? It is often said that they do, and commentators have given names such as 'Redemption through Love' to the lyrical motive that is prominent in the last moments of the work (a motive that has been heard once before, in *Die Walküre*, when Siegfried's conception is announced). But this, like all other names of motives, is their invention, and it is less justified than many such names. Although throughout his works Wagner is fond of words that mean something like 'redemption' and applies them generously to various situations of cleansing, or restoration, or forgiveness, or justification, or merely release, no words that suggest a redemption of the world appear among the several things that Brünnhilde addresses herself to in those last moments.

The gold, of course, is now purified, because it has been returned to the Rhine – the only place, as the Rhinemaidens sing at the end of *Rheingold*, for what is trusty and true: 'Traulich und treu ist's nur in der Tiefe.' The gold, if one insists on the word, has been redeemed. But there is no suggestion that the gold's return, or these deaths, have also redeemed the world, at least if that means that the world has become a better or freer place. The future, at the end of *Götterdämmerung*, is plainly not a concern at all. This is an embarrassment to the political interpretations of the *Ring* which started with Shaw and have been particularly popular since the 1980s, in many versions ranging from the illuminating to the merely opportunistic. They all begin with a great impetus from *Rheingold*, with its manifest images of expropriation, self-impoverishment and slavery, but even the most resourceful of them tends to peter out as the cycle proceeds, finding material at its end only for some vapid hope for a politics of innocence.

The problem with this is not that the *Ring*, as it proceeds, simply avoids politics. It is rather that the hope for a politics of innocence is what it centrally rejects. If one wants transportable philosophical conclusions from the *Ring*, and Wagner himself insisted that one should not want any such thing, one of them will be that there is no politics of innocence, because nothing worth achieving can be achieved in innocence. Only in the depths, where nothing has been imposed on Nature or wrested from it, is the trusty and true. Siegfried is as near to pure Nature as any active human being can be, and he eventually achieves nothing but disaster. Wotan does achieve many things, but in deep lack of innocence. Forced back from doing (in *Rheingold*) to manipulating (in *Walküre*) to leaving Siegfried free, he chooses to accept his own end in the hope of achieving something by purely innocent means – that is to say, by leaving everything to a purely innocent agent. *Götterdämmerung* shows how this does not work; and, particularly through the incident of the Rhinemaidens' refusal of the ring, why it could not work. Human action is significant only if it expresses knowledge, and knowledgeable action is already distanced from pure innocence.

It has been said that the direction eventually taken by the *Ring*, as contrasted with *Siegfrieds Tod*, represents a shift from optimism to pessimism: Wagner said it himself, describing his earlier state of mind, a little strangely, as one of 'Hellenic optimism'. But it has also been denied, and the denial, too, is correct: both sides in this old debate are right. This is not because the *Ring* is a muddle. No doubt it is, in certain ways, a muddle, but it is not because of its muddles that it can be seen as expressing pessimism and, equally, as rejecting it. That is due to the elusive demands of pessimism itself. What counts as pessimism or optimism is a question that can be pressed at several different levels, and the *Ring* itself helps to make that clear.

At one level, the mere recognition that there is no innocent politics might be regarded as pessimistic. At a more interesting level, however, it is only after this truth has been recognised that alternatives of optimism or pessimism really come into question. In this perspective, the difference between thinking that there can be an innocent politics, and that there cannot be, is not a difference between optimism and pessimism, but between fantasy and reality. If we start from that point, optimism or pessimism will be seen as attitudes to the life that human beings can live within the borders of reality, borders already set by the imperfection, suffering and confusion that are necessarily involved in any large-scale enterprise. The question of pessimism or its reverse will then be: granted that this is the reality of life, is it worthwhile?

There is more than one way, however, of thinking about what might make it worthwhile. Hegel and Marx, for instance, agreed (only too eagerly, some have thought) that the course of history could not be innocent, but they believed that its crimes and sufferings could be vindicated by its outcome: that it would reach a final state in which history was transcended and the cost of it all would have been justified. A historicist or teleological optimism of this kind is represented in Wagner's political aspirations of 1848 and, perhaps, in *Siegfrieds Tod.* That, certainly, he gave up.

Yet there is still another question beyond this, which Nietzsche, for one, saw as the real question of optimism or pessimism: even if life and history have no justifying end, even if the crimes and miseries are never in that sense paid for or cancelled out, could it, entirely in its own terms, have been worthwhile? It is at this level, finally, that the *Ring* raises the question, and at this level its reply is 'yes'.

It is indeed often said that Wagner, at some such level, was a pessimist too, above all because he associated himself with the philosophy of Schopenhauer, which not only rejected progressivist readings of history but regarded all willing as painful, unsatisfiable and empty. Wagner did not read Schopenhauer until after he had written the *Ring* poem, but when he did he saluted Schopenhauer as a great thinker, just because he expressed ideas and attitudes that Wagner claimed to have formed already in his own experience. One can get into complex arguments about possible intimations of Schopenhauerian ideas in the *Ring*. It is said that one can see in such terms Wotan's renunciation of his own existence. But Wotan does not renounce his existence because of some metaphysical insight into the nature of action, but as a last stratagem for bringing about what he wants – a stratagem that involves not only (like many stratagems) leaving things alone, but leaving them altogether. Moreover, it is agreed that in embracing his own and the gods' end, Wotan performs an act of heroic renunciation; but how can such an act issue from cosmic weariness and

disillusion? It makes no vast demands on heroism to give up an existence
that one has come to see as totally worthless.

To pursue such arguments runs the danger of treating the *Ring* as though
it were a philosophical text. We may be tempted to do so, because Wagner
himself, like most of his principal characters, was so relentlessly self-
expository. One may be trapped into arguing with his words, because he
wrote so many of them, both in his dramas and about them. But it is a
large mistake. What matters is the work itself, and when one turns back
to that, it is obvious that the *Ring* defeats, at this most basic level, a
pessimistic interpretation, not because of what it says but in virtue of what
it is. What the work conveys is that the process of trying to create an artificial, human, order out of Nature, granted all its costs and its eventual
failure, is worthwhile simply in its own terms. The *Ring* expresses this
because it elicits as it moves towards its end a cumulative sense of its own
complexity, power and achievement.

What this expresses is not (and it is very important that it is not) the
idea that life is redeemed by art – the idea that real life, and real suffering,
cruelty and humiliation, are justified because they can issue in great works
of art. It is doubtful that Wagner believed this even about his own works.
It is not that the splendours of the *Ring* can justify real life. Rather, the
Ring's celebration of what it has presented can symbolise for us ways in
which life may celebrate what life has presented.

It is in some such way that we must understand the peaceable and
healing presentation of ultimate disaster in *Götterdämmerung* and, above
all, its celebration, in the funeral music, of the seemingly uncelebratable.
The funeral music is totally retrospective in its effect, and it is essential to
our experience of the *Ring* that it should be so. It is offered as the celebration of the life, just ended, of a great hero. Yet the individual subject of
this shattering musical memorial scarcely exists. In *Götterdämmerung*,
certainly, the great hero has done nothing that we can take seriously as
heroism, and we have been involved more deeply for much of the cycle
with Wotan, a much greater character than he. A strain or awkwardness
over this point might be explained by the adaptation of *Siegfrieds Tod* to
the purposes of the *Ring*. But the important point is that there is no strain.
If we respond to the *Ring* at all, the funeral music will work on us at least
as powerfully as anything in the cycle. How can this be? To say that it is
because of the music is to say nothing, since this is dramatic music, and it
makes sense at this point only if it makes dramatic sense. It makes sense

because we hear it as the celebration not of a man but of a process, of all that has gone before in the *Ring*.

In 1872, the year in which he finished composing *Götterdämmerung*, Wagner wrote an essay in which he revised the theory of music drama that he had set out earlier and admitted what he had previously denied: the primacy of the music. In this essay, he said that he might almost describe his dramas as 'deeds of music made manifest'. Those deeds of music cannot in themselves justify the world of compromise and cruelty, but they can express what it would be like for it to be justified, because they invoke a state of mind in which, at least for a while, the world can seem to justify itself.

9

Wagner and the Transcendence
of Politics

1

How should we think about Wagner? Those who are troubled by that question, as I am, presumably think that as an artist he is worth being troubled about: that his works, or some of them, are demanding, inviting, seductive, powerful. Not everyone who cares about music need share that opinion. The relation of Wagner to the history of Western music and to the formation of a taste is not the same as that of, say, Bach or Mozart: he is not in the same way necessary. His works are indeed necessary to explaining its more recent history, very obviously so, but they are not in the same way a necessary part of a taste for Western music. Indeed, it is possible for a serious music lover to hate them – but that is not really the main point, since hatred can be a reaction to their power, in particular because of the peculiarities I shall be discussing. So Thomas Mann referred to Nietzsche's 'immortal critique of Wagner, which I have always taken to be a panegyric in reverse, another form of eulogy'.[1]

You can have a well-formed, deep relation to Western music while passing Wagner's works by, finding them boring or not to your taste. But it is clear, equally, that a passionate engagement with these works is not a mistake or a misunderstanding. They are amazing, and there is much to engage with. It is no accident not only that Wagner is voluminously discussed but that immense efforts, expenditure and imagination are still devoted to producing these pieces.

As well as the troubled and the bored and the revealingly hostile, there has notoriously been a further party, of the utterly devoted, and perhaps there still is. Being devoted does not necessarily mean being uncritical, but if the members of this party are critical, it is on the very local basis that the Master did not always live up to his own standards. This party has a question to answer. No-one can deny that some of Wagner's own attitudes are ethically and politically disturbing, some of them very deeply so. I mean that they are disturbing to us; and by that, I mean that they are rightly found disturbing by people who have seen the crimes and catastrophes of the twentieth century. We do certainly have to understand his attitudes in the context of his time, taking into account the options and ideological contrasts that were available then. We need to understand what his attitudes meant. But, equally, we have to take into account what they have come to mean.

When it is said that 'we have' to take such things into account, one thing this means is that we have no alternative if we are not to be misunderstood. In Shakespeare's *Much Ado about Nothing* (V.iv.38), Claudio says, 'I'll hold my mind [i.e. stick to my intention to marry her], were she an Ethiope.' In the Norton Shakespeare, the editor, Stephen Greenblatt, gives an explanation: 'In other words, black and therefore, according to the Elizabethan racist stereotype, ugly'.[2] A review in the London *Sunday Times* criticised him for this on grounds of excessive political correctness. But as Greenblatt reasonably said in an interview, would they have actually preferred it if he had said, 'black and therefore ugly'? In Wagner's case, 'we have no alternative' does mean this, but it means something else as well: that we have no alternative to taking into account his attitudes and what they have come to mean if we are to experience and reflect on these works at the depth they demand – more precisely, if we are to understand them at the level needed for them to become a significant part of our experience. (Indeed, so far as staging is concerned, we have to take these things into account if we are to put these works on at all, and this is a point I shall come back to.)

If we try to understand as a genuine historical question what range of opinions and attitudes was available in Wagner's world – 'where he was' on various matters – we find that in some cases, he was already in a pretty bad place. Above all, and most notoriously, there is his anti-Semitism. His article 'Das Judentum in der Musik', attacking Meyerbeer and Mendelssohn and, generally, the artistic impotence of Jews, did not make a big stir when it was first published under a pseudonym in 1850. The document had considerably more effect when he reissued it under his own name in 1869, with additions in an even sharper tone and with more directly racist implications ('so far from getting rid of his errors,' Liszt said, 'he has made it worse'). The racist emphasis, influenced by Gobineau, was prominent in other publications of his last years. It has reasonably been claimed that Wagner by his own writings contributed to the resurgence of anti-Semitism in Germany in the 1880s, in particular by helping to make it culturally respectable.[3]

Moreover, it was not only during the Nazi time, through the friendship of Wagner's daughter-in-law Winifred with Hitler, that the Bayreuth Festival, which Wagner founded in 1876, became associated with the most repellent ideas. The house journal, the *Bayreuther Blätter*, was founded in 1878, when Wagner was still alive, by an acolyte, Hans von Wolzogen, who, as an historian of the festival has put it,

> used the journal as an ideological instrument to propagate a racist, anti-Semitic, chauvinistic, xenophobic and anti-democratic ideology. It would be difficult to find anywhere in the Western world in the late nineteenth century, even in the darkest corner of the French right, a publication so poisonous, so hate-filled, so spiritually demented.[4]

In some other cases, the attitudes that Wagner held were capable of taking more benign forms, but Wagner's versions were not among them. This seems to be true of the particularly chauvinist form that he gave to the idea that there should be a German art.[5] Thomas Mann considered this in his famous essay (from which I have already quoted) 'The Sorrows and Grandeur of Richard Wagner,' which, given as a lecture in 1933, led directly to his exile from Germany, and which is, along with some of Nietzsche's thoughts, still the most helpful reflection that I know on these questions.[6] Mann pointed out, using a distinction made by a Swedish writer, that Wagner's aspiration was for a German art in the sense of *nationale Kunst* rather than *Volkskunst* – that is to say, the nationalism was a matter of the destiny and political significance of German art, not of its materials.

This in itself may seem an entirely intelligible, even innocent or laudable, nineteenth-century ambition. But then we have to recall that the problem of a distinctively German art, and its relation to a self-conscious artist working in a broader European tradition, had been a preoccupation of German thought since at least the late eighteenth century. Above all it had been a recurrent concern for Goethe, with regard to the German language, its traditions of writing, the public for that writing, the self-conscious cultivation or rejection of differences from the rest of Europe, the relation of German art to various possible political regimes in the German-speaking states, and so on. Indeed, in his writings on these subjects Wagner, unsurprisingly, praises Goethe and Schiller.

Now the German world in the 1860s was certainly a very different place from what it had been in 1800. Yet it is still relevant to point out that in Goethe's case the question of how to achieve a distinctively German art was a problem *for him*, a problem to which he responded in ways that honoured its complexity; whereas for Wagner it was, of course, a problem to which, at any given stage of his career, he knew the answer, as against the traitors and enemies who took a different view. This absence of the Goethean spirit, not just in a form anachronistic by the 1860s, but in any form at all, is something I shall come back to when we confront the impression, not lightly to be dismissed, that for all their wonders and power there is an all-consuming assertiveness in Wagner's works which can be disgusting.[7]

I have moved directly from talking about Wagner's personal attitudes, as expressed in his writings, to talking about the character of his work. That is not an oversight; the problem is that the two cannot entirely be separated. It is possible that artists with politically disturbing views could produce works that are not politically disturbing. There are without doubt several things wrong with Hans Pfitzner's remarkable opera *Palestrina* (first produced in 1917), such as its heavy-handed attempt to present the Council of Trent in the style of *Die Meistersinger*; but they do not express what was wrong with Pfitzner himself, whose conservative and nationalist views were congenial enough to the Nazis that (to his great resentment) he was required to undergo denazification after the Second World War. Wagner's relation to his works was not like this. That is obvious now and has been obvious since they were created, but we shall have to ask what it is about the works that makes this so.

What is troubling is that the problems raised by his repellent attitudes on the one hand and by the disturbing power of his work on the other cannot be solved by a distinction between 'the work' and 'the man'. Or rather, we cannot immediately call on that distinction to solve them. The problems that matter of course concern the work: it is only the fact that we want to take the work seriously that forces us to confront Wagner at all. But it does indeed force us to confront him, because Wagner's is a case in which, if we are to deal adequately with the work and its power, we have to take into account the attitudes of the man and what they have come to mean. I do not mean that his views, even his views of his own works, necessarily determine our interpretation of them. His works are independent, in varying degrees, from the outlook expressed in what he wrote around and about them, but we have to ask in every case how far they are independent of it, and in what ways. We need to understand, in particular, how far what moves us in the work may be connected with what frightens and repels us in his attitudes.

Some contemporary approaches to the work, though they are very vocal about Wagner's attitudes, fail to grasp that this is the question, and fall short of what we need in order to think about it. A lot of writing about Wagner since the 1970s conceives the problem as that of revealing a hidden scandal; the authors try to trace the ways in which the attitudes have marked the works.[8] These writers spend a lot of effort, for instance, in trying to find signs of anti-Semitism in the operas themselves, claiming that the representations of Mime, Klingsor, Beckmesser and other characters introduce Jewish stereotypes. I am not concerned with the question, still much disputed, of whether the attempts at decipherment of these characters are correct. Even if a nineteenth-century audience did not need as much help in recognising such stereotypes as, seemingly, we do; even if Wagner consciously intended them (for which there is no direct evidence); the point is that these supposed signs are too trivial to help with the only question that can reasonably concern us. The only reason for worrying about Wagner's works is that they are powerful and interesting. But if that is so, what difference would these signatures, these local coded messages, make?

In effect, these writers reduce the problem of Wagner's anti-Semitism (so far as the works are concerned) to these supposed traces, to the idea that, in one instance or another, Wagner is knowingly signalling it. This cannot help to deal with any deep anxieties caused by Wagner's works. In fact, it serves to reconcile these writers' admiration for them with their bad conscience about his attitudes, but at a painless and superficial level. They have externalised the problem, moving it from where it truly belongs.

We can take an analogy from a quite different work of Thomas Mann's, *Death in Venice*: these critics treat the threat, the dangerousness, of Wagner as if it were the outbreak of cholera, which with luck you can signal and confine by whitewashing and disinfecting the walls. But our, and their, real problem with Wagner is not like this at all – rather, it is like Aschenbach's problem with Tadzio. These critics do not accept at the right level the way in which Wagner is related to his works. They are saying, in effect, that there had *better* be something wrong with the works, and they have come up with a circumscribed and relatively painless way of identifying what this is.

In a well-known book Robert W. Gutman has written,

> Unhappily, a proto-Nazism, expressed mainly through an unextinguishable loathing of the Jews, was one of Wagner's principal leitmotifs, the venomous tendrils of anti-Semitism twining through his life and work. In his final years, his hatred reached out further to embrace those with black and yellow skins. This attitude cannot be shrugged off as an unfortunate whim or a minor flaw in a musical hero.

This underlines the point that the presence of some anti-Semitic signatures is not in itself enough: they are not going to show that anti-Semitism is 'one of [the] principal leitmotifs' of Wagner's work. The works will have to be more thoroughly polluted than that, and in his book Gutman gives interpretations to suggest that they are (though he does less to show that these interpretations are inescapable). But then he is thrown back to the question of why these thoroughly polluted works are supposed to be interesting or important to us. To this, his answer appeals simply to the music:

> Yet Wagner survives, and primarily because he was a great musician. His ripe late-romantic style retains much of its allure. . . . A music of almost unparalleled eloquence and intimacy keeps his works on the stage.[9]

This is not an answer at all. Having refused to separate the man and the work, Gutman tries to separate the work and its music, an aim which can be seen to be failing already in the use of words such as 'eloquence' and 'intimacy,' and which is anyway peculiarly hopeless in the case of Wagner, who took unprecedented steps to unify musical and dramatic expression. If we end up with such an evasion, it is clear that we must start again.

2

Some modern productions of Wagner's works have another way of trying to 'externalise' the problems. It is a significant fact that we have seen in the opera house in recent years the coexistence of two kinds of radicalism. In cases to which it is appropriate, there is an increasing 'authenticity' of orchestral and vocal performance, based on historical research; and at the same time there are productions and sets which display all degrees of rethinking and creativity up to the now notorious extremes of directorial whimsy – which themselves are more or less what has come to be expected.

These two developments might seem to go in opposite directions. It is true, of course, that they can conflict, as when the production makes it impossible for the singers to express what the music requires or invites them to express. (It is important that this should not be described as a conflict between music and drama; it is a conflict between the dramatic contribution of the music and the dramatic contribution of the staging.) But this is a matter of particular failures, not of what is intrinsic to the two kinds of radicalism. Even quite extreme versions of them, if they are put together in the right way, can produce a triumphant success (this was true of Peter Sellars's 1996 production at Glyndebourne of Handel's *Theodora*). They can combine to the same end. The musical performance tries to offer a closer approximation to the composer's means of expression; the production offers a version of what this drama, these emotional relations, can mean in terms that make sense to us now – it tries to find visual and dramatic equivalences, which work for us, to the expressive content both of the words and of the music as that music is now presented to us. No theatrical presentation of the drama that was simply determined by historical research could possibly do that.

In fact, the idea of a theatrical production of an opera which is 'authentic' in the sense in which musical performances can aim to be 'authentic' (and that itself, of course, raises large questions which are not the concern here) seems to be virtually nonsensical. Critics who attack what they see as the extreme innovations of recent directors and call for 'traditional' productions of the *Ring* cannot mean that we should be given what Wagner in 1876 in Bayreuth actually had – for one thing, we know what Wagner thought of what he got in 1876.[10] But quite apart from that, since the question is one for us, of what we should do, even the most devoted intentionalist will have to ask not what Wagner wanted granted the resources he had, but what he would have wanted if he had had our resources; and that means of course, also, resources to present his works to audiences who have seen what we have seen (and not only on the stage). We are back, unsurprisingly, where we started, with the problems of staging

Wagner's works for us now. In pursuit of a truthful production, there is absolutely no alternative to re-creation.

The objection to some recent productions of Wagner is not that they are in a new idiom, but rather that they do not use that idiom to re-create. What some of them offer is mere comment. Unlike the decipherment of the supposed anti-Semitic signatures, which I have just considered, the ideologically critical treatment of the works in these productions is not minor or episodic. Their comments may be continuous, as when Wotan is throughout represented as a tycoon in the 2000 Bayreuth production of the *Ring*. The problem arises if they are no more than comments, external to any response to the content of the works; in that case, they are like the supposed decipherment of anti-Semitic messages.[11] Just as being given a decoding of Beckmesser's vocal style as Jewish, even if it were correct, would do very little to help one understand or shape one's reactions to *Die Meistersinger*, so a continuous subjoined ethical health warning added to the *Ring* – the mechanical injection into it of modern hate-figures, for instance – does not help one to face what the *Ring*, both for good and for bad, requires one to face.

We have to address the works and the problems they present on a larger scale. We have to ask: what general features of Wagner's style contribute to the problems? I should like to suggest three, all of them characteristics that were mentioned by Thomas Mann.

Wagner shared with other nineteenth-century artists, notably Ibsen, the aim of uniting the mythic and the psychological. One might even suggest – this is my suggestion, not Mann's – that in a certain sense Wagner is Ibsen inside out. Ibsen succeeded in some of his works in taking realistic bourgeois domestic drama and giving it the weight, the sense of necessity, that one can find in Sophocles; Wagner took myths and medieval epics and installed in them a psychology which is often that of bourgeois domestic drama. There is a basic problem with this enterprise, implicit in Walter Benjamin's observation that the heroes of ancient tragedy or epic lack an inner life in a modern sense: many, if not all, of those ancient works gravely express a necessity that transcends biographical particularity. To reconcile this fact with a drama for which intensity almost unavoidably means intense subjectivity is a hard undertaking, as many nineteenth- and twentieth-century artists have found.

In fact, there are three levels involved. Besides the mythical or medieval materials, and the explicit motivations and situations of bourgeois drama,

Wagner engages in depth-psychological explorations which are expressed in words and music that go far beyond naturalistic drama. Wagner is most successful in reconciling the mythical and the psychological, so it seems to me, when it is this last element that prevails: when the subjective intensity is so extreme, solitary and unrelated to citizenly or domestic life that in its own way it takes on an authority which is perhaps analogous to that of ancient tragedy. This is notably so in *Parsifal* and in Act III of *Tristan*. Elsewhere he succeeds because he can sustain an analogy with domestic drama which does not need to apologise for itself: an obvious example is Act I of *Die Walküre*.

Sometimes the analogies are imperfectly negotiated, and even the 'arts of transition' of which Wagner was justly proud cannot hold the levels together. I personally think that this is true, at all three levels, of King Mark's recriminations in Act II of *Tristan*. There is the problem that the view of the lovers from an everyday social perspective is less interesting at this point than what we have just experienced inside the world of night that they have entered; and in addition, for all the references to heroes and courtly honour, it is hard to dissociate Mark's complaints from a bourgeois embarrassment, doubtless familiar to Wagner himself. In such cases there are problems for production, but with skill and luck they can be dealt with. However, there is one central case, the character of Siegfried, in which there is a real vacuum, a collapse at the heart of the work, and the very questionable conception of heroism which is associated with him has, I am going to suggest, a political significance.

Another, and very manifest, feature of the style is that Wagner really did break down in some ways the conventional distinction between the musical and the non-musical. As Mann put it, while the old criticism that Wagner's music is not really musical was absurd, nevertheless it was not entirely unintelligible: Wagner's work does in a way fuse the musical and the literary. Mann says about the E flat chord that starts *Das Rheingold*, 'It was an acoustic concept: the concept of the beginning of all things. Music has been here pressed into service in an imperiously dilettante fashion in order to represent a mythical concept.'[12] This implies that the 'deeds of music made manifest' which, as he was finishing the *Ring*, Wagner said were offered in his work,[13] and the psychological/ethical/political signifi-cance of the text (or rather, one should say, the action), can only be under-stood in terms of each other. It is no peculiarity of Wagner that what the work means is not given merely or primarily by the action: it is true of all opera, or at least of all great opera. But Wagner's style does make the dramatic relations between music and action at once more pervasive and emotionally more immediate. We have already seen one consequence of this, that one cannot adequately explain the power of Wagner by simply appealing to the music. There is another consequence, in (so to speak) the opposite direction: that if someone feels that there is something ethically or politically suspect about, in particular, the *Ring*, that feeling, whether it is correct or incorrect, is not going to be met simply by appealing to the action or, more narrowly, to the text.

It is a paradox that some defenders of Wagner, having elsewhere extolled the unity of music and text in his works, think it is enough to meet these ideological criticisms by pointing out that, according to the plot, oath-breaking and theft do not pay off. Whatever the hopes may be for recovering an overall sense of the end of the *Ring*, you are not going to find it in its closing words, and it is a significant point, a point which comes back again to the figure of Siegfried, that one of the most overwhelming and also, I am going to suggest, unnerving episodes of *Götterdämmerung*, the funeral music, has no words.

Wagner is, more than any other, a 'totalising' artist; in any given work, all the elements relate to one underlying conception or tone. Mann, once more, puts this very well, in terms which, from a technical point of view, are no doubt exaggerated, but which express something entirely recognisable:

> It is this infinite power of characterization that . . . separates the works from each other, and develops each of them from a basic sound which distinguishes it from all the others; so that inside the totality of the *oeuvre*, which itself constitutes a personal world, each individual work again forms a self-contained unity, like a star.

Nietzsche said that in any given work of Wagner's it is as though it were all presented by one impersonator with a very distinctive voice; and, since the biographical presence is also strong, this impersonator may easily be taken for the composer.[14] All doubt, duality or underdetermination is either internalised into the action (the characters are represented as undecided or in conflict), or it is externalised, existing outside the work altogether (the work stands against the rest of the world); doubt and duality do not exist at the level at which the work offers itself. The work itself voices or implies total unity and certainty. Because the voice of the work is so distinctive in Wagner's case, and, once again, the historical presence of the composer is close (for instance in suggesting what the whole enterprise stands against), the sense is not of a world assumed, but of an outlook asserted.

The extreme modernism of Wagner's later style implies that he is not taking for granted the ethical or social assurances which give structure to many other confident dramatic works of the nineteenth century, such as those of Verdi. But at the same time, though he represents ambivalent characters and actions that have ambiguous or perverse consequences, he was not disposed in the least to the typically modernist development by which ambivalence and indeterminacy become part of the fabric of the presentation itself, so that it is essential to the work that it does not finally tell its audience what to make of it. There are few operas, in fact, that have achieved this effect, but they include two of the greatest among twentieth-century operatic works, *Pelléas* and *Lulu*.

3

I come back to the absence of the Goethean spirit that I mentioned earlier in connection with *Die Meistersinger* and the project of founding a German art. Part of the suspect quality of Wagner lies in the fact that although he portrays conflicts and contradictions, such as Wotan's indecisions, his recognition that he cannot directly achieve what he wants, the tensions between power and love, and so on, Wagner's tone in presenting these things seems to have at each point an indomitable assurance. He is telling us what it all adds up to. This aspect of Wagner's style can produce fear and resentment; one can have the sense of being locked inside Wagner's head; and it can also give a sense of fraudulent manipulation. Moreover, as soon as Wagner's assurance – the feeling that he thinks he has a hold on what is unconditionally significant – encounters the political, particularly in his trying to transcend it, it can become deeply alarming.

These features and the reactions they arouse may mean that some of his devices simply do not work. But sometimes Wagner's inventions work when it seems that they should not, and then our resistance (and hence our conflicts) can be especially strong. More than one consideration that has already come up leads us to particular and very central examples of this, the funeral music in *Götterdämmerung*, the orchestral interlude between the scene of Siegfried's death and the final scene of the whole

Ring. The funeral music is almost entirely retrospective in its effect, and it is essential to our experience of the *Ring* that this should be so. No-one, I think, could describe it as regretful, or melancholy, or resigned. It is manifestly triumphant. It is offered as the celebration of the life, just ended, of a great hero. Yet, as many critics have noticed, the subject of this shattering musical memorial scarcely exists as a person.

Siegfried is the least self-aware, in every sense of the word the least knowing, of Wagner's heroes. He does not know much about anything, least of all about himself, and a lot of what he does know he forgets for most of *Götterdämmerung*, under the influence of Hagen's drug. Although, in his dying moments, the memories of his love for Brünnhilde are restored to him, they do not bring with them any greater understanding, but only a return to a blissful past. In this, and in his relation to these magic drinks, he is quite unlike Tristan, who in his great monologue in the third act comes to see how everything that has happened flowed from himself. To Siegfried, on the other hand, the machinery of spells remains external, and represents nothing in his motivations or his wishes. If he had any character at all, it would be only a limitless – one might almost say clinical – guilelessness.

His encounter with Brünnhilde did teach him something, fear. This gave him, we are told, a new experience, but it is notable that we are not given much more than the telling of it. There is a good deal of psychological material in the last scene of *Siegfried* after Siegfried awakens Brünnhilde, and it is of course expressed in the music, but it almost entirely concerns Brünnhilde's transition from warrior to lover. Siegfried as lover gets new music, but very little of a new psychology. What he carries forward from the encounter is nothing but a blissful memory; and when he reasserts his individuality as a hero and returns to the world of action, there is no project for him except action itself. 'Zu neuen Taten!' ('New deeds!') is the first thing that Brünnhilde says to him in *Götterdämmerung*, and, if we take it for granted that he is to resume the only life he is able to live, there is nothing else for her to say. What matters is the absence of an inner life, not in itself the absence of intelligence. Parsifal is defined by a holy lack of intelligence, but in the course of the action he gains an inner life; the confrontation with memory and sexuality that is enacted in such extraordinary terms in the second act changes him completely, whereas to Siegfried nothing significant happens at all.

It is not impossible for a great hero to lack an inner life: as Walter Benjamin pointed out, the heroes of epic and ancient tragedy are often presented with a notably reticent indication of their subjectivity. But it is much harder to present as a great hero one who is simply naïve and unimaginative, and whose great deeds, the slaying of the dragon and the journey to Brünnhilde, are not so much emblems of courage as the products of an infantile fearlessness. This is no Achilles. He appears, moreover, in a drama in which subjectivity, self-consciousness, reflection, personal ambivalence and so on are pervasive, expressed in the artistic means themselves, and, above all, central to the existence of another character, Wotan, who has a better claim to be the hero.

Because the celebration represented by the funeral music is of the seemingly uncelebratable, there is a crisis of theatrical production at this point. Recently we have often been given an empty stage or Siegfried's body lying undisturbed. On the occasions I have seen them, these came out as lame or desperate devices; but it is not surprising that there is desperation. Critics complain of a wilful, contemptuous rejection of the heroic. But it is not the directors' fault that there is a failure of the heroic. They are reacting, if inadequately, to a feature of the work which, if it is allowed to emerge, is bound now to seem empty or potentially alarming.

Since there is this dramatic failure, it is a real question why the funeral music can indeed be effective, in fact overpowering; and it is not enough to say that it is an astonishing piece of music, since it is a piece of dramatic music in the deepest Wagnerian sense. I think that there is an answer to the question of how it can move us so much, and I shall come back to this. But the problem that comes first, one that is signalled by the directors' difficulties, is that of heading off a different kind of message – an implicitly political message – which can readily fill the gap left by Siegfried's absence as hero. I said that the funeral music, granted that absence, can be alarming. The reason for this lies in its relation to the political, or rather, unpolitical, aspects of the *Ring*.

The serene and reconciling motive that appears in the last moments of *Götterdämmerung* used to be called 'Redemption through Love'. None of these labels for the leitmotifs has any authority, but this was worse than most. For what, even in Wagner's overgenerous use of such words, has been redeemed? Brünnhilde of course sacrifices herself by riding into Siegfried's funeral pyre, but if this is to count as redemption, rather than suttee on horseback, it has to have some further result. She says, 'This fire, burning my frame, cleanses the curse from the ring.' Indeed, the gold is now purified, because it has been returned to the Rhine – the only place, as the Rhinemaidens sing at the end of *Rheingold*, for what is close and true: 'Traulich und treu ist's nur in der Tiefe.'[15] The gold has been redeemed, if one insists on the word. But there is no suggestion that the gold's return, or the deaths of Siegfried and Brünnhilde, have also redeemed the world, at least if that means that the world has become a better or freer place. The future of the world, at the end of *Götterdämmerung*, is plainly not a concern, while the gods have no future at all. This is an embarrassment to the familiar political interpretations of the *Ring*. They all begin with a great impetus from *Rheingold*, with its manifest images of expropriation, self-impoverishment and slavery, but even the most resourceful of them tend to peter out as the cycle proceeds, finding material at its end only for some vapid aspiration to a politics of innocence.

The problem with this is not that the *Ring*, as it proceeds, avoids politics. It is rather that the hope for a politics of innocence is one thing that it seems to reject. If one wants transportable lessons from the *Ring*, a conclusion to be drawn from the story of Wotan will be that there is no politics of innocence, because nothing worth achieving can be achieved in innocence. Only in the depths, where nothing has been imposed on Nature or wrested from it, is the tender and true. But the nobility and grandeur of the funeral music stand against this. Not because of what it says (it says nothing) but, all the more, because of what it does, it can carry the suggestion that perhaps there could be a world in which a politics of pure heroic action might succeed, uncluttered by Wotan's ruses or the need to make bargains with giants, where Nibelungs could be dealt with forever: a redemptive, transforming politics which transcended the political.

Such ideas had in Germany a long, complex and ultimately catastrophic history. Politics, or at least 'ordinary' politics, the politics of parties, power, bargaining and so on, was seen as something divisive, low, materialistic and superficial, in contrast to something else which was deep, spiritual and capable of bringing people together into a higher unity: something, moreover, which instead of peddling satisfactions, demanded renunciation and suffering. There were two main candidates for this higher thing, art and the nation, or, indeed, the two together.

Such ideals informed the influential conception of the *Sonderweg*, the idea of a special path that German development might follow, distinct from (in particular) Britain and France; and one expression of the difference lay in a supposed contrast between *Kultur*, which was German and deep, and *Zivilisation*, which was shallow and French. (Thomas Mann himself had supported such ideas during the First World War, and still in part sought to justify them in the diffuse work which he published in 1918, significantly called *Betrachtungen eines Unpolitischen* ('Reflections of a Non-Political Man').)[16] All the elements of this tradition were to be exploited in a desultory but ruthlessly opportunistic way by Hitler.[17] Hitler was far from unpolitical, but he pretended to be, and perhaps himself believed that in him the nation had transcended politics: that the politics which brought him to power and which, together with terror, kept him in it was indeed a politics of transcendence.

Wagner was certainly deeply committed to the nationalist ideals of the *Sonderweg*, but it is rare in his works (as opposed to his writings) that the will to transcend politics points in a distinctively political direction. *Die Meistersinger* certainly has political implications; as Nietzsche rightly said, it is against *Zivilisation*, German against French. Moreover, it invites questions, which it notably fails to answer, about the politics of art. Hans Sachs believes in the judgment of the *Volk*, and in the last scene the young knight Walther gets their enthusiastic approval, with a composition which, we are told, reconciles inspiration with tradition. Wagner no doubt thought that the same could truly be said of his act as a whole. But in fact nothing in this bland formula, or in the way it is worked out in *Die Meistersinger*, is going to close the gap between Wagner's intensely radical avant-garde experiments and music that could be straightforwardly popular as, for instance, Verdi's was.

The politics of art – the relations of Wagner, his music and the German people – remain at the end of the opera an unsolved question. But the relation of all this to politics in a narrower sense, the politics of government, is not even a question in *Die Meistersinger*. Although in the last moments of the work (in a notably obtrusive passage, which Wagner seems to have put in at Cosima's insistence) Wagner gets Sachs to declare the ideals of artistic nationalism, he is careful not to commit himself to what its political implications might be. Sachs's last words on the subject are 'Even if the Holy Roman Empire dissolved in mist, yet there would remain holy German art!' And this in its context can fairly be taken to say that the ideals of German art can survive, even if politics change radically or go badly wrong. This might be called the avoidance of politics.

With *Parsifal*, the one work that Wagner wrote after he had completed the *Ring*, the situation is different again. Nietzsche was clearly wrong when he said that Wagner had ended up by prostrating himself in front of the

Christian cross. Wagner did nothing of the sort: roughly speaking, he took some coloured snapshots of the Eucharist and used them to illustrate his journey into the psychology of sex, guilt, memory and pain. (He thought that Nietzsche lacked a sense of humour, because he presented him with a copy of the *Parsifal* poem inscribed from 'Richard Wagner, Oberkirchenrat' – as it were, 'The Right Reverend Wagner' – and Nietzsche did not find it funny.) But the work does undoubtedly steal some of its resonance from Christian ritual and its associations, and in particular, Wagner's recurrent theme of a redeemer sustains in this case much of its familiar religious meaning. Indeed, in the magnificent climax to Act III, Gurnemanz, crowning Parsifal as king, uses language so dense with references to redemption and salvation that it has even been suggested that he is addressing not Parsifal but the Redeemer Himself.[18]

Although Parsifal becomes a king, he is not a king over any subjects. Nor does the opera suggest that mankind is reclaiming its identity from religion, as in the more Feuerbachian moments of the *Ring*. Here we can speak of a genuine absence of politics. What we have is the exploitation of religious remnants in the interests of a drama that operates almost entirely at the level of depth-psychology. This involves a kind of trick, because in places the work has to pretend that the whole of human life is transcended and justified by something higher (as it is represented in the final scene, indeed, literally higher), the Holy Spirit. But the psychological material is so powerful, the symbols of the wound and the spear are strong enough, and, above all, the musical invention is so compelling that Wagner's *Allmacht*, his capacities as a magical manipulator, enable him just about to get away with it. The director is left with some nasty problems, but we need not be, and certainly not any that have to do with politics.

It is not an objection to *Parsifal* that at the time of writing it Wagner wrote increasingly crazy articles tying its story together with themes of racial purity. It might be, for some people, an objection to going to see *Parsifal*: they might feel that they did not wish to be associated in any way with a work written by a man with such an outlook. That is, as people say, their privilege. But it has nothing at all to do with interpreting or responding to *Parsifal*, because whatever theories Wagner may have had, they do not structure the work, or surface in it, or demand our attention in experiencing it.

When Robert Gutman, for instance, says, 'Parsifal's sudden insight in the magic garden was the realization that by yielding to Kundry he would dilute his purebred strain', he is not reporting the plot, the text or any implication of the music's associations. He is simply saying how it might look to someone who thought about little but Wagner's racist writings. My point here is not to reinstate the distinction between the work and the man, which I have already said is not a helpful device in Wagner's case. The point is just that one cannot decide in advance, either positively or negatively, what facts about the man, his views and their history may be relevant to responding to a given work. In particular, if we acknowledge its power, it is a question of what it is in us that does so, and in the case of *Parsifal* we have a good enough idea of what that is to know that it has nothing essentially to do with Wagner's racist ravings.

In *Die Meistersinger*, politics is avoided, and from *Parsifal* it is merely absent, but with the *Ring*, neither of these is true. The cycle emphatically addresses issues of power, and if at its end it suggests that the world in which they arise is overcome, it is hard not to be left with the feeling that the questions of power and its uses have not so much been banished as raised to a level at which they demand some 'higher' kind of answer.

I said earlier that there is an explanation of why the funeral music can move us so much even when we recognise that the supposed object of its triumph does not exist. I suggest that it makes sense because we hear it as the celebration not of a man but of a process, of all that has gone before in the *Ring*. The *Ring* as it moves towards its end elicits a cumulative sense of its own complexity and power, and it is this that the funeral music celebrates. The music itself helps to bring this out, as motives associated with earlier parts of the story come to the surface. In celebrating its own fulfilment, the work can make us feel that the whole disaster-laden history has been worthwhile.

What this expresses is not – and it is very important that it is not – the idea that life is redeemed by art, the idea that real life, and real suffering, cruelty and humiliation, are justified because they can issue in great works of art. It is doubtful that Wagner believed this even about his own works. It is not that the splendours of the *Ring* can justify real life. Rather, the *Ring*'s celebration of what it has presented can symbolise for us ways in which life even in its disasters can seem to have been worthwhile. In these terms the *Ring* emerges as what it should be, an affirmative drama, and not in a way that invokes a hypothetical and deeply suspect politics of heroism and sacrifice.

The problem still remains, however, whether the part that Siegfried plays in the story can, on any adequate reading, bear the weight that it is required to bear. Some of the strains in the work come, without doubt, from the complex changes of mind that Wagner underwent as he wrote it. But the problem is not just that the work is imperfect. What really matters is a product of history, that the strains pull us towards a sense of the work in which the transcendence of politics tends to suggest not the absence of politics, but a higher, transcendental, politics, of a peculiarly threatening kind.

This is signalled by problems of theatrical production, and those problems remain even if we come to hear the funeral music as a tragic affirmation rather than the celebration of an embarrassingly non-existent hero. The questions that emerge concretely as problems for the theatrical director are in any case questions for all of us, if we do not allow Wagner's extraordinary ingenuity to deflect us from them. Particularly with regard to the *Ring*, but not only there, it may be impossible, even in our imagination, to re-create Wagner's works altogether adequately. It may be that the total unity of psychology, myth and morally redemptive significance to which Wagner aspired is an illusion, not just in the sense that it is unattainable – that is true of Beethoven's ideals of freedom – but because, as Nietzsche said, it is based in some part on a pretence that a set of theatrical, often grandiose, gestures can reveal the nature of the world. If that is so, then to that extent no honest treatment of it can make it work as a whole. We can do it justice – but then it comes out guilty of that pretence, and justly associated, for indelible historical reasons, with a politics that has since Wagner wrote moved into the gap left by that pretence. Or it can come out less guilty – but then theatrical re-creation will have negotiated this as an accommodation between historical memory, what Wagner tried to bring about, and what we can now, decently and (as we say) in all honesty, accept.

If, at least for some of Wagner's works, a production which 'did them justice' would find them guilty, this will constitute the historical vengeance of the ethical on an artist who uniquely raised the stakes high enough for such a vengeance to be even possible.

Notes

1. 'The Sorrows and Grandeur of Richard Wagner', in *Pro and contra Wagner*, trans. Allan Blunden (London, 1985), p. 100. (In quotations from Mann, I have sometimes modified the translation.) Nietzsche's attacks on Wagner certainly represent an ongoing deep fascination with him, but some of his remarks may also strike a chord with those who

are less involved: 'My objections to Wagner's music are physiological objections. What's the point of dressing them up in aesthetic formulae?'

2. New York and London, 1997.

3. This is argued by Jens Malte Fischer in a helpful and admirably balanced introduction to an edition of Wagner's pamphlet, *Richard Wagners 'Das Judentum in der Musik:' Eine kritische Dokumentation* (Frankfurt am Main and Leipzig, 2000). For a review of Wagner's anti-Semitism, see the article by Dieter Borchmeyer in *A Wagner Handbook*, ed. Ulrich Müller and Peter Wapnewski, translation edited by John Deathridge (Cambridge, Mass., and London, 1992).

4. Frederic Spotts, *Bayreuth: A History of the Wagner Festival* (New Haven and London, 1994), p. 84. According to Cosima's diary, Wagner did once tell Wolzogen that he wanted the journal to strike a broad, idealistic note, and keep away from 'specialities', such as vegetarianism and agitation against the Jews. See Cosima Wagner, *Die Tagebücher*, 2 vols (Munich and Zürich, 1976–77), vol. 2, p. 700; cited by Fischer, p. 118.

5. His article 'Deutsche Kunst und deutsche Politik' (first published anonymously in a newspaper in 1867, then in book form in 1868) can be 'interpreted, at least in part, as a commentary on *Die Meistersinger*', according to John Deathridge in *The New Grove Wagner* (London, 1984), pp. 52–3. I come back later to the question of whether *Meistersinger* is itself expressly political.

6. There is one significant qualification to be made: that neither in this essay, nor (yet more remarkably) in pieces written during and after the Second World War, did Mann, so far as I know, mention Wagner's anti-Semitism.

7. It was a 'nameless presumptuousness' in wanting to have something to say about every-thing that Mann particularly had in mind when he said in a letter to Emil Preetorius of 1949 that 'there is a lot of Hitler in Wagner'.

8. For instance: Robert W. Gutman, *Richard Wagner: The Man, His Mind, and His Music* (London, 1968); Hartmut Zelinsky, '"Die Feuerkur" des Richard Wagner oder die "neue Religion" der "Erlösung" durch "Vernichtung"', in *Richard Wagner: Wie antisemit-isch darf ein Künstler sein?* (Munich, 1978); Barry Millington, *Wagner* (London, 1984); Paul Lawrence Rose, *Wagner: Race and Revolution* (London, 1992); Marc A. Weiner, *Richard Wagner and the Anti-Semitic Imagination* (Lincoln, Nebr., and London, 1995). The idea goes back at least to Theodor Adorno, *Versuch über Wagner*, written in 1937–8, first published as a whole in 1952; English translation by Rodney Livingstone, *In Search of Wagner* (London, 1981.)

9. Gutman, *Richard Wagner*, pp. xiv, xviii. It is ironical that Gutman drops a conde-scending sneer towards Wagner's early biographers for their 'Victorian delight in bringing ethical standards to bear on artistic affairs'.

10. Wagner did very much like the *Parsifal* that he got in 1882, apart from a problem with the moving scenery. See *Wagner on Music and Drama*, selected by Albert Goldman and Evert Sprinchorn from translations by H. Ashton Ellis (London, 1970), pp. 369–76. It would certainly look very strange now.

11. It is perhaps worth saying that I do not think that this criticism applies to Patrice Chéreau's 1976 Bayreuth production of the *Ring*, which is widely known on video (issued by Philips). Some of its inventions are gratuitous, but for the most part it embodies extremely sensitive responses to the drama.

12. As Adorno pointed out (*In Search of Wagner*, p. 28), the idea that Wagner was a 'dilettante' goes back to Nietzsche's essay 'Richard Wagner in Bayreuth', written at the time of the first festival in 1876.

13. In the essay 'Über die Benennung "Musikdrama"' (1872).

14. *Nietzsche contra Wagner* (Leipzig, 1889), 'Wo ich Einwände mache'.

15. In Andrew Porter's translation, 'Goodness and truth dwell but in the waters.' See Richard Wagner, *The Ring of the Nibelung* (London, 1977).

16. Trans. Walter D. Morris (New York, 1983).

17. The presence of this among other cultural legacies in Nazi discourse, and above all in Hitler's own speeches, is the subject of J. P. Stern's fascinating book *Hitler: The Führer and the People* (London, 1975).

18. See Lucy Beckett, *Richard Wagner: 'Parsifal'* (Cambridge, 1981), pp. 52–3.

10

L'Envers des destinées

Remarks on Debussy's *Pelléas et Mélisande*

When Debussy's *Pelléas* was first performed, on 30 April 1902, the public reaction on the whole was one of disappointment. It was felt, at first, even by some of the more advanced critics; there was a feeling that the work was too thin, too shapeless, too indefinite. Rimsky-Korsakov voiced a widespread view when he said that the 'harmonic combinations were incomprehensible, the orchestra lacked body and firmness of texture, the whole was monotonous; and he could see no future for this "curious experiment"'.[1] As many writers have said subsequently, the reactions of that first audience have to be understood in the light of their Wagnerian expectations. Admittedly, a deeper insight into those harmonic combinations, original as they were, would have seen how firmly they were rooted in the experiments of *Parsifal*: Debussy's great struggles to leave Wagner behind had led, harmonically, to radical development and change rather than to rejection. But in terms of melody and of dramatic conception, the rejection was thoroughgoing, and his textures deliberately moved away from what he called 'Wagner's American opulence'.[2]

'I do not feel tempted to imitate what I admire in Wagner,' he wrote; 'my conception of dramatic art is different. According to mine, music begins where speech fails. Music is intended to convey the inexpressible . . . I would have her always discreet.'[3] 'I hate the leitmotiv,' he is reported to have said, 'not only when it is abused, but even when it is used with taste and discernment. Do you think that in composition the same emotion can be expressed twice? In that case, either one has not reflected, or it is simply an effect of laziness. I should like to see the creation – I, myself, will achieve it – of a kind of music free from themes and motives, or formed on a single continuous theme, which nothing interrupts and which never returns on itself.'⁴ The crucial remark in this is, I think, the one about the same emotion not being expressed twice: while there are, as critics have eagerly pointed out, certain motives, of a fleeting kind, in *Pelléas*, they never label, nor even more tactfully serve to take us back, to remind us of anything: they genuinely form at each occurrence a new emotional compound.

'I would have music discreet': some have felt that discretion has too strong a hold on *Pelléas* – and some, in performance, have made it so. Some have found it possible to appreciate the wonderful rhythmic subtlety of the accompaniment, the extreme refinement of the scoring, and yet feel that too high a price has been paid for this, in terms of dynamic energy. The point was inimitably put by Richard Strauss, whose reactions to this effete Gallic production were vividly set down by Romain Rolland: Strauss said, 'C'est très fin, très ... (he gestures with his fingers) très *gekünstet*; mais ce n'est jamais spontané; cela manque de *Schwung*' ('It's very subtle, very ... very artful, but it's never spontaneous: it has no oomph')⁵ – a remark, incidentally, notably expressive of that sophisticated vulgarity which was to become the hallmark of Strauss's own art.

But the objections went beyond a decadent overrefinement of style. The work was called enervating, invertebrate, morbid, pernicious: 'Existing as it does with the minimum of vitality,' one critic wrote, 'it tends to impair and destroy our existence. The germs it contains are ... of decadence and death.'⁶ Here we have a reading of the style – a profoundly wrong one, in my view – which is conditioned by an equally wrong reading of the dramatic content. Profoundly wrong: the power of *Pelléas* lies not just in mysteriousness or delicacy, but in a great humanity. It offers a representation of its characters' inner life which is uniquely subtle in opera, and it does not do that in order to express an enfeebled excess of sensibility. Rather it offers a certain picture, a strong picture, of what in the inner life is most alive, and of what in the way of tenderness and imagination is needed to keep it alive.

But to see how *Pelléas* does that, we first have to get out of the way a view of the work which indeed represents it as enervating – and, by influencing production, can make it seem so. This is the view that the work is all about inescapable fate and that the characters are all passive victims; a view which in its best-known form places the work in the world of Edgar Allan Poe. Both Maeterlinck and Debussy followed Baudelaire in being strongly impressed by Poe. Edward Lockspeiser has gone so far as to say that 'the underlying inspiration of *Pelléas*, both the drama of Maeterlinck and the opera of Debussy, derived from Edgar Allan Poe and in particular *The Fall of the House of Usher*.[7] Now Debussy was certainly, throughout his life, fascinated by that tale. Before *Pelléas*, in 1890, he is said to have been writing a symphonic work based on the story. Later, the project of making it into an opera occupied him, on and off, from 1908 to the end of his life; and he produced two versions of a libretto for it. He is reported as having said that Poe 'had the most original fantasy among the literature of all lands; he found a note absolutely new and different'.[8] Something in that 'sense of mystery and the passion for the beyond' which Maeterlinck felt he got from Poe may have helped to attract Debussy so instantly to the drama when it was first performed in Paris in 1893; though also, no doubt, he had a sense that it was exactly what he needed for his conception of opera, that it was in a certain sense incomplete, that the play was, as Mallarmé said of it, an opera without music.[9] But it seems to me strained, in relation to Debussy at least, to see as Lockspeiser does the old castle in the kingdom of Allemonde ('all the world') as Usher's decrepit residence; and downright perverse to see Pelléas, the eager Pelléas who wraps himself in Mélisande's hair, the *child*, as Golaud (though only with half-perception) calls him – to see him as 'pale and feeble and overcome by destiny' . . . a reflection of Usher, the quintessential man of an over-refined civilization'. There are indeed one or two traces in the libretto of Poe's fascination with the charms of approaching death. Pelléas's father, we are told, said Pelléas had the grave and friendly face of those who will not live for long; and famously, Pelléas says to Mélisande, 'you are strangely beautiful when I kiss you so; you are so beautiful one would think that you were going to die'. Though worthy of an honourable place in a Vincent Price movie, those lines are not near the heart of what *Pelléas* is about.

The theme of overwhelming fate, or an inert belief in the hopelessness of all action, is not the point. Debussy implied a more vigorous view when he said, once more in the context of explaining his rejection of Bayreuth, that what he wanted for libretti were 'poems that will provide me with changing scenes, varied as regards place and atmosphere, in which the characters will not argue, but live their lives and work out their destinies'.[10] There is emphasis in the story of *Pelléas* on the *imperfection* of action, because of the characters' lack of understanding of it; but it is to trivialise this, and to lose its tragic quality, if one reduces it to a blank, external and preordained fate. One is specially overimpressed by the theme of fate if one places the centre of the play's truth in the character of Arkel: who belongs, Debussy said, 'to the world beyond the grave, and is full of the disinterested and far-seeing affection of those who are about to pass away'.[11] But impressive, resigned and exceedingly ancient though he is, he is not omniscient, nor should we take him as the measure of all the action, rather than as an important contrastive element in it. 'At my age,' he says, 'perhaps the surest fruit of my life, I have acquired a certain faith that one can rely on events' – 'je ne sais quelle foi à la fidélité des événements': a vaguely reassuring phrase which, like his earlier thought that there may be no utterly useless happenings, in fact gives us no insight into the events of the opera at all, but is rather itself shown up, ironically, as quite inadequate to them. Confronted with the scene of intense brutality in which Golaud throws Mélisande about by the hair, and then, suddenly and hysterically quiet, says, 'I shall leave it to chance', Arkel offers the one thought, 'if I were God, I should have pity on the hearts of men'. We are not compelled to regard this as a very deep comment on what has happened; in fact it is probably as well to admit the plain truth, that it is utterly idiotic.

But there is one of Arkel's sage observations which comes nearer to the heart of this work: when he says, and it is practically the very first thing he says, that we see only the back of destiny, even of our own: 'nous ne voyons jamais que l'envers des destinées, l'envers même de la nôtre': the *reverse* side, as a piece of tapestry or other cloth has a reverse, or wrong side. So we do see *something*, but what we see is the wrong way round, and also fragmentary, gaining a sense only from a different point of view. So we can only imperfectly understand what we or others do; and there is a problem indeed, faced with the reverse side, not just of knowing what the pattern is, but of knowing whether what we take to be parts of a pattern really do contribute to a pattern at all – whether there is anything, in a given area, which responds to our guesses or questions. There is a problem about which questions may have answers, and which have no answers at all. What the opera tells us is that to many of the questions that we are driven by our fears to ask about ourselves and others, there are no answers; and that it is essential to the life of the feelings to recognise that fact.

Mélisande, famously, is surrounded by unanswered questions, from her first appearance. And when she gives answers, they often fail to meet the questions that were meant. 'Has someone hurt you?' asks Golaud, at their first meeting; 'Yes, yes, yes' – 'Who?' – 'Everyone.' – 'What did they do? – 'I will not say, I cannot say.' – 'Where did you come from?' – 'I ran away.' Further questions, equally unanswered, are suggested to us, as by the

crown which has fallen into the water, the crown which 'he' gave her –
who? These questions without answers do not serve merely to generate a
sense of vague mysteriousness: they provide, further, the thought that if
there are answers, they could not explain or have anything usefully to do
with things as they now are. But beyond that there is a further sense, that
certain questions have no answers at all – that they are asked under a
misunderstanding, to the effect that reality is determinate, is there to be
described, in ways in which it is not. It is this sense that comes to the fore
when Pelléas starts to question Mélisande, in their first scene by the fountain, before the ring is lost: and before he learns, as he tacitly does learn,
that questioning may not find out anything – something which Golaud, in
a way which forms the centre of the tragedy, can never understand. 'Why
didn't you want Golaud to kiss you?' Pelléas asks: 'Oh, oh,' she says, and
points out something she saw in the water. The accompaniment, tuned
here as in so much of the work to the smallest movements of the mind,
expresses the troubling of its surface, as of the water. And when the ring
has fallen in the well, and she asks what she is to tell Golaud, Pelléas in the
last line of the scene replies, 'La vérité, la vérité' – words which echo
hollowly against the fact that even the bare happening she cannot tell him;
because of the deeper fact that if there was any real truth about that occasion, it did not consist in that bare happening. It is the notion of a determinate truth about Pelléas and Mélisande that Golaud so obsessionally
and destructively pursues: even, terribly, to her deathbed in the last act,
where that word, 'la vérité', is hammered out again and again; and even
then when Golaud gets answers, he does not have answers to the questions
he meant. 'Did you love Pelléas?' – 'Why yes, I loved *him*. Where is he?' –
'Don't you understand? ... were you guilty?' – 'No, we were not guilty,
why are you asking me this?' And then in his brutal insistence on being
told, he fails to notice or care that *he* is telling *her* something, that she is
going to die.

Linked to the central idea of a truth which is not to be had in the terms
that Golaud understands are the contrasting images of blindness and
sight, and of darkness and light, which run through the work. The ancient
Arkel is nearly blind, but not entirely so; but Golaud, his desire for his
truth finally frustrated, will die 'like a blind man'. 'It is no use asking,' he
says at the end, with Mélisande dying, 'she is already too far from us': irony
indeed that Golaud should think *that* is the problem, when in the scene of
his assault on her he could learn nothing, and was driven mad by learning

nothing, from her great eyes, although he was 'so close to them that I could feel the breath their lids made in closing'.

The most desparate enactment of Golaud's need for what he supposes would be knowledge is that scene, at the end of Act III, in which he first questions the child Yniold about Pelléas and Mélisande, and then lifts him up to look into her room. Once again it is questions, insistent questions, and first they get answers, but tantalising answers, which run obliquely to what Golaud wants to hear: but then the child is frightened, the reflecting surface breaks up, and there are no answers at all.

This very subtle, but also very frightening, scene lays bare the difficulty in staging *Pelléas*, a difficulty which is very real: among the great master-pieces of the operatic stage, I think it may well be the hardest to present. The difficulty lies in keeping the edge on Golaud's questions, the human pain that goes into their being asked, while preserving the sense that they do not have, at any important level, answers, that no reality corresponds to them. Go one way, and one has a mysterious haze, with music indeed sensuous and marvellously structured, but losing human and dramatic interest: go the other, and one is left with the irritable feeling that there must *be* a truth there, and it is a tiresome and accidental limitation that we and Golaud do not know what it is. The performance must not let us be seized by Golaud's conviction – that if one could get into little Yniold's point of view, one would *learn* some vital thing.

Golaud is standing in the dark, trying to see what is in the light, using the eyes of a child. But he, of all people, is not capable of using the eyes of a child; if he were, he would not be doing what he is doing. He lacks vision because he is both too old and not grown-up enough. For him Pelléas and Mélisande are children; he repeatedly and with increasing anxiety assures himself that their relations are those of children, and after the killing, in the last act, he falls back briefly and unconvincingly on this: they kissed like little children, brother and sister. But his image of childhood itself is blankly simple, like his image of innocence: they both involve lack of what he would count as knowledge. And Mélisande does lack what he would count as knowledge, since she is not at all knowing; but her innocence (if that is what it is) can be on very level terms with honest understanding, as when she says to Pelléas in the last scene of Act IV, 'I only lie to your brother.'

Golaud's idea of the childlike is only that of the childish, and the crude betrayal implicit in that is displayed when, in the second act, he sternly reminds Mélisande that she is not a child – when he encourages her to adjust herself to this dark castle in its black forest, where everyone is old; joy does not come every day, he says to an accompaniment of ultimate desolation; and he tells her that she is too old to weep at not seeing the sky.

But where the sky and light are, is the air, also, and the sea. They represent life; and not to weep at not seeing the sky is not to care about having died. The sense of air and the light of the sea is very powerful in this opera. So, in the last scene of the first act, where, after talk of the sombre forest round the castle, 'Look round that side, look the other way,' Mélisande is told, 'and you will see the light of the sea': and then darkness falls, and the ship departs, the ship which brought Mélisande there (another unanswered question); and then, as the wind rises on the sea, Pelléas takes Mélisande by the arm, for her hands are full of flowers, to help her down the dangerous path – their first physical contact.

This scene gains, and gives, further resonance when it is compared with the scenes in the third act in which Golaud and Pelléas go down to the vaults of the castle, and return again to the air. Now, it is Golaud who takes Pelléas by the arm, not the hands, as he leans over the cleft: but with a different wish. The darkness and suffocation here are the expression not only of Golaud's murderous wish, but of his ignorance of it; the return to the air is the escape, not only from death, but from self-deception. It is marvellously realised in the music – almost too insistently, perhaps, in the interlude between the scenes, which, like all the interludes, Debussy added at the last moment.

Apart from the interlude, these scenes were composed early on, in 1894. 'The scene in the underground caverns was done,' he wrote to a friend, 'filled with subtle terror, and mysterious enough to give vertigo to the best-inured soul! And also the scene on leaving those same caverns, filled with sunlight, but with sunlight bathed by our good mother the sea.'[12] The return to our good mother the sea, and to the light, is the return from secret destructive wishes; but it is not the return to perfect knowledge, if we mean by that, that to every question we have, under the sky, an answer. Rather, what we have there is a freedom from questions, or at least, from the wrong questions: what darkens, blinds and suffocates is not just ignorance, but the ignorant insistence on knowing, the attempt to determine the indeterminate: what lives in the light with open eyes, dies when it is clubbed with the demand for *la vérité*.

To this basic complex of themes, one scene must present a very special problem: the declaration scene at the fountain, the last of the fourth act, where Pelléas and Mélisande reveal their love to one another. For at this point the language of suggestion and indirection, both verbal and musical, has to give way to something more like direct statement; and so subtly has the sense of indeterminateness been created, that there must be a difficulty about what, exactly, that statement will be *of*. We know that Debussy had trouble with this scene. His work on it dates from the very beginning, in 1893, but he destroyed a first draft. 'It isn't at all right,' he wrote. 'It's like a duet by . . . anyone at all. Worst of all, the ghost of old Klingsor, alias R. Wagner, appeared at a turning in one of the bars. So I tore up the whole thing and set off in search of some more characteristic compound of phrases . . . I have quite spontaneously utilized a medium which seems a rather unusual means of expression, namely silence (don't laugh).'[13] And the scene is famous for the orchestral silence which accompanies, so to speak, the words 'Je t'aime' – 'Je t'aime aussi.' Justly famous, for it is very effective, but the critics' emphasis on it, understandable when *Pelléas* was particularly seen as an anti-Wagnerian opera, can distract attention from other things which seem, in the context of this utterly original work, rather conventional; after the silence, and again after the closing of the gates has shut the pair out of the castle, the idiom comes for a moment or two dangerously close to the world of Massenet.[14]

It seems significant to me that there is room for doubt here. For Debussy has created in the work up to this point an image of the inner life and its indirect relation to understanding, so extraordinary and original that none of the ways in which total explicitness can be used in opera is available to him. It is not just the sound of *Tristan* (in particular) which has to be avoided, or its length, or its loudness, but the whole idea of any convention by which the inner life is expressed totally, without qualification, and on the authority of the composer. So over these words, at this moment, it is not surprising that one should sense a certain artifice. But even if that is true for a page or so, the end of the same scene achieves a deep and upsetting effect, absolutely in keeping with the work, when in Golaud's attack it presents a culminating image of blind ignorance. The most moving *silence* in this scene is perhaps not, after all, that of the orchestra, but of Golaud, as he plunges through the dark to destroy what he does not understand, and what is not even there to be, in his terms, understood.

Notes

1. Oscar Thompson, *Debussy: Man and Artist* (New York, 1967), p. 174.
2. In a letter to Ysaÿe: see Léon Vallas, *Claude Debussy: His Life and Works*, trans. Maire and Grace O'Brien (Oxford, 1944), p. 274.
3. Vallas, p. 84.
4. The remark was reported by André Fontainas: see Thompson, pp. 102–3, for the whole account of Debussy's remarks at a Symbolist evening.
5. See Edward Lockspeiser, *Debussy: His Life and Mind*, 2 vols (London 1962, 1965), vol. 2, p. 90, n. 2.
6. Camille Bellaigue: Vallas, pp. 127–8.
7. Lockspeiser, vol. 1, p. 195.
8. Thompson, pp. 203–4.
9. See Lockspeiser, vol. 1, Appendix E.
10. Thompson, pp. 121–2.
11. Vallas, p. 86.
12. Thompson, p. 128.
13. Vallas, p. 86.
14. Joseph Kerman *(Opera as Drama*, New York, 1956, p. 190) has expressed a doubt about this scene, pointing out that it is the one place where Debussy is tempted to expand his musical material.

Manifest Artifice

The Ingenuity of Puccini

The criticism of operas, as distinct from the criticism of performances, is still not a very developed activity. Insofar as it exists, it has tended to concentrate on discussing the music, rather than operas as dramatic and musical wholes. The fact that there is not much serious criticism of Puccini's operas is not, therefore, necessarily surprising. But such criticism as there is has tended to be hostile or contemptuous, and I suspect that, in this particular case, the lack of serious comment is itself a comment. Puccini is not taken entirely seriously.

At the same time, several of his works are, of course, tirelessly successful with the public, and this is not hard to explain: they are, at their best, immensely and almost indestructibly effective. This fact is sometimes used as a humbling rejoinder to critical doubt – 'so there'. In itself, it is not enough of a rejoinder, but it raises a demand, at least, for more understanding.

We perhaps tend to assume too easily that we understand Puccini, the character of his work and his place in the history of opera. In fact, he is not easy to place. It is not obvious, for instance, what comparisons it is useful to make with him. If one merely looks around him, to Leoncavallo, or Mascagni, or Giordano, he of course stands out, and his powers of lyrical invention seem magical. If one looks back to Verdi, Puccini becomes a small figure – but then not only was Verdi a great genius, but it was inconceivable that after him anyone could achieve anything of similar scale in Italian opera.

More interestingly, one can look sideways, to Richard Strauss, and indeed there is enough stylistically in common for a certain kind of now rather tired lyricism to be called the 'Puccini-Strauss' style. But they had very different aims and origins. In Italian opera, there was still such a thing as straightforward popular success, and Puccini aimed at it; while Strauss, as a German composer after Wagner, wrote orchestrally complex operas to Expressionist or Symbolist texts, as well as being a composer of 'serious' music outside the opera house. Strauss was, almost by definition, a more 'serious' composer than Puccini. But it is far from clear that as an opera composer he should therefore be taken more seriously.

Such comparisons in fact effect nothing until one has taken a closer look at what Puccini tried to do, and the individual musico-dramatic methods that he employed. Puccini is no doubt a limited artist, but his limitations, and the failings of his works, are themselves markedly individual. *Tosca* is at the centre of the problem of getting a clear and balanced view of Puccini. Of all his pieces it is one of the most famous for its theatrical effect. It is also distinctly nasty, in a way which helps to bring out critical hostility; in fact, it defines a central form of hostility towards the composer, since the touch of nastiness is typical of him, and *Tosca* presents the best-organised example of it. *Butterfly* is also nasty (particularly in the first version, which failed and which has only recently been revived) but it is much more sentimental, and the overall effect is of pathos rather than cruelty. *Turandot* is even more sadistic than *Tosca* – to the extent that, to permit the torture of Liu, the hero's behaviour has to be made barely intelligible – but it is musically more ambitious, and it has the undoubted appeal that it defeated him: for once, Puccini was not so insufferably on top of it all.

Tosca is not perfect, even in its own terms, and it is more flawed, perhaps, than *La Bohème*. 'Vissi d'arte' is a not very interesting piece which, as Puccini himself later came to feel, holds up the action. In Act III, Cavaradossi's nostalgic solo before the dénouement, 'E lucevan le stelle', leaves a desultory impression and seems not to contribute enough to the significance of the action. I suspect that in part this is because, like some other Puccini tenor arias – 'Nessun dorma' in *Turandot* is an obvious example – it is simply too short, and makes the effect of one shouted sentence rather than any revelation of character. The words of this aria replaced, at Puccini's insistence, a heroic set of reflections on life and art which, we are told, attracted Verdi's favourable attention when he was shown the libretto. Puccini found that he could do nothing with these, and set instead a reverie on past love-making. That fact in itself is not the cause of the weakness of the scene. Puccini is writing a different kind of work, and in some ways a more modern work, than any to which those heroic reflections would have been appropriate. Cavaradossi, like some other Puccini characters, is a man of softly impressionable sexuality – qualities already clearly expressed at the beginning of the opera in the aria addressed to his painting, 'Recondita armonia'. He seems to be a revolutionary hero largely by accident, and his involvement in the action is a good deal more personal than political. Even more striking than 'E lucevan' in this direction is his reaction to Tosca's telling him that she has murdered Scarpia: he comes out with the sentimental and very pretty 'O dolci mani', which sweetly turns its back on anything that such a murder might mean. These pieces weaken the third act, as Puccini's publisher, Giulio Ricordi, indeed complained. They do so not because they are personal and sexual rather than political, but because they do not move anything forward, or contribute any further dimension to what is going to happen. Especially in relation to Puccini's insistence on compressed and rapid action (which he got, presumably, from Verdi), these static moments can seem simply opportunistic – particularly since 'O dolci mani' has one of those Puccini melodies that encourage tenors and conductors to reckless amounts of rubato.

There are, then, weaknesses in *Tosca*, even in terms of Puccini's own conception of how it should work. But the interesting thing about *Tosca* lies in its suspect strength, in the fact that not only is it operatically successful, but it is a fundamental example of operatic success. It thus raises a question, not just about Puccini, and the special character of his achievement, but about the nature of opera itself.

There are a few basic ways of being excited and held by the operatic stage. The trio in the last act of *Rosenkavalier* represents one, and 'Di quella pira' in *Trovatore* another. *Tosca* at its best displays several. The end of Act I, for instance, with its mounting excitement and its superimposition of a great dark baritone declamation onto the rhythm of a tolling bell and religious ritual, is a splendid example of something that real opera lovers really love. *Tosca*'s continuous success with the public is not a mere triumph of bad taste or a result of contemporary associations, as has been the case with certain works of Meyerbeer, or Gounod, or Menotti. What is compelling in *Tosca* has direct connections with what is compelling in greater operas.

It is hard to think of a parallel to this in non-musical drama. Leaving aside questions of the limitations of his purely musical invention, the critical resistance to Puccini lies principally in the conviction that there is something manipulative or even cynical about his work. That conviction is, in my view, basically right. But that leaves the problem, since these manipulative works resemble, in their capacity to hold us, operas which have no such faults. If opera is at all a serious business, how can this be? This is *the* question about Puccini, and its answer lies in what it is like to experience opera.

Auden's remark that 'the singer may be playing the role of a deserted bride, but we feel quite certain . . . that she is having a wonderful time' makes the essential point that 'the enjoyment of opera – and it is particularly true of Italian opera – grows tightly round enjoyment of a technique, a *manifest* technique.'[1] Here there is an interesting comparison with, and an important difference from, conventions of the non-operatic stage. When people who do not care for opera and know nothing about it ridicule the convention of conversation in song, it is right to remind them of other theatrical conventions, in particular the conventions of conversation in blank verse, which they may be less inclined to reject. In watching Shakespeare, one indeed appreciates it as verse – at least, if the director allows one to. Excitement, tension, involvement, are generated by that verse, and by its being verse, but in the opera house it goes further than this. It is not only song, and the fact that it is song, that generates excitement, but the singer. At a fine operatic performance, we are conscious of the singer's achievement and of the presence of physical style and vitality, and the sense of this reinforces the drama itself. A concrete feeling of performance and of the performers' artistry is nearer the front of the mind than in other dramatic arts. It is because of this that outbreaks of applause (if not, these days, the granting of encores) can be appropriate, as they scarcely could be with a play, even one in verse.

Puccini's immense success is connected with the fact that the pleasures of opera, particularly in the Italian style, are in any case involved with an obvious and immediately presented artifice. He was of course ingenious (Toscanini said, 'Puccini is clever, but only clever'), and he was greatly gifted in the creation of theatrical atmospheres and gestures – atmospheres and gestures which *announce themselves* as theatrical. In Act I of *Tosca*, the threatening arrival of Scarpia is synchronised with the climax of the horseplay between the sacristan and the choirboys, in a way which precisely draws attention to itself as a musical and dramatic device. Similarly, the opening of the third act offers a complex and sophisticated texture of bells and a shepherd boy's song which heightens the tension for what is to follow. These effects heighten it in a specially self-conscious and indirect way – by making one aware all the time that this has been conceived as a preparation for what is to follow.

Again, in the second act, Scarpia's arrangement of his treachery gives pleasure through the very theatricality with which it is displayed. His instructions to Spoletta tell him, but not Tosca, that the execution of Cavaradossi is to be only a pretended fake, that the 'simulated' killing is to be a real one. 'As we did in the case of Palmieri,' says Scarpia, more than once: 'You understand?' 'Yes,' replies Spoletta, as he leaves, 'like Palmieri'. It is appropriate that the subject of this should be a double falsehood, a pretence of a pretence. It is not simply a device of dramatic irony, which puts us into complicity with them against Tosca. It puts us into a complicity with that device itself, with a certain tradition of theatrical effect, and it is in seeing the wheels of artifice turn that we enjoy it.

The idea which Puccini carries further than any other opera composer is that of securing an effect through the audience's consciousness that that is what he is doing. In exploiting this idea, he transfers to the level of musical and dramatic invention something that is always inherent, to some extent, in opera, and the performance of opera; and that is why one can acknowledge the truth of his talent to the nature of opera.

That acknowledged display of artifice, which is Puccini's most characteristic device, is not of course enough to secure his popularity. For that he needed, what he outstandingly had, melodic gifts, orchestral ingenuity, a sense of atmosphere and a talent for compression. But, granted all that, the peculiarity of his talent does specially define the nature of the popularity that he achieved. In particular, it affects what it is like to see one of his operas with which one is already familiar. With a very great work, to hear it for the twentieth time gives the chance, not just to hear something one has missed, but to understand something new. That is not the point with Puccini, and everybody knows that it is not the point. The aim is, rather, to see him do the trick again; the better one knows the whole thing, and the more familiar the trick, the greater the pleasure, just because the pleasure lies in complicity with his artifice. One enjoys the entry of Scarpia very much more when it is not a surprise – that is to say, when one is not actually surprised by it, but rather knowledgeably looks forward to the effect of the surprise.

It is sometimes held against Puccini's operas that they are melodramatic, but that is certainly not the notable or exceptional thing about them. As the word itself implies, it is hard for operas of strong action to be anything else, and many operatic masterpieces are melodramatic: *Rigoletto*, for instance, or, in good part, *Fidelio*. The special characteristic of Puccini's operas is that they are manipulative – that in place of the direct address of those two works, for instance, or indeed of any work of Verdi's, there is a calculated, and indeed displayed, contrivance to produce a certain emotional effect. The highly conscious and self-referential character of his method is a very modern feature of Puccini's work, and he could not have stood anywhere but at the end of the tradition of Italian opera, extracting the last drops from it by the method of openly exploiting our consciousness of the ways in which it produced its effects. At the same time, what is achieved through this sensibility is limited – or at any rate defined – by a certain lack of expressive ambition, both musical and dramatic. In his use of swift narration, schematic characters and deftly indicated moods, together with his self-conscious exploitation of familiar conventions, Puccini is a cinematic artist, and some of the most natural comparisons that his works invite are with films. Use of a popular melodic style and the conventional directness of his narrative provoke comparisons not with 'art' films of, say, German Expressionism, but with the finest products of the Hollywood studios in their best days – which indeed, like Puccini, learnt some of their technique from more ambitiously innovative art works. It would be a mistake to take this as an insult to Puccini: these films are so excellent that the comparison gives no reason to underestimate his operas, but merely offers a better perspective from which to enjoy them.

Like many good Hollywood film-makers, moreover, Puccini found it natural to use distant, unreal or fantasy subject matter. In this his operas also resemble, of course, many other operas. But in Puccini's case, something special is effected by the choice of subject. The fact that Verdi's works are remotely placed (with the famous, and at first disastrous, exception of *La traviata*), and that Wagner's are often placed nowhere at all, imposes in itself no limit at all on their power or honesty or significance. But in Puccini's case, there is something suspect about the exoticism of the oriental pieces, and the fanciful quality of *Bohème*'s Parisian life. They provide an element of distancing, a way in which the work can be exciting or touching without being disturbing. Hollywood constantly used such methods, though it could also – in some of the crime films, for instance – go beyond them.

Here again, *Tosca* is the central and the test case. *Tosca* is, in fact, the exception, the one really twentieth-century subject among Puccini's major works. It is totally unimportant that it is set in Napoleonic times. It really asks to be set in the twentieth century, above all in Mussolini's Italy, with Scarpia as a Fascist boss. Many things in the opera fit such a time and such a régime, including the character of the villain. Scarpia's corruption, and the sense, which I have already mentioned, that Cavaradossi is a man with other interests who got into it all by accident, conspire to make the torture scene more a psycho-sexual event than anything political, and this is a recognisably modern motive, of a kind inconceivable, certainly, in Verdi.

Yet it is just here, where Puccini gets close to a disturbing reality, that his method of exploiting the traditions of Italian opera rather than trans-forming them ceases to work, and the displayed artifice stops being any longer an acceptable source of pleasure. He was very skilful, for the most part, in avoiding that situation, by taking an exotic or fanciful subject matter, or very schematically indicated situations of horror or pathos. (It is ironical that 'verismo' should be the name given to some of these devices.) A danger always lay for him in the real strength of his fascina-tion with violence, what he himself called his 'Neronic instinct'. In some cases, notably *La fanciulla del West*, he channelled it in a direction of schematic fantasy which leaves room for his devices to work. In at least one case – parts of *Turandot* – the obsession rises above the devices.

In the second act of *Tosca*, however, his sadistic imagination pulls too strongly on what is indeed one of his most carefully structured pieces of artifice. The effect is one that many have found disturbing and disagree-able, and much more so than some other operas which contain, in terms of their action, equally brutal material. The careful placing of Cavaradossi's off-stage cries gets its effect, like the earlier use of Tosca's off-stage concert, once more through the consciousness of artifice: the music invites us to hear the effect being created. But the tension has been suffi-ciently raised, Scarpia is enough of a figure, the subject is close enough to reality, for pleasure not to run easily through such craftily constructed channels. Puccini's best effects come about through the manifest *use* of feeling, of circumstance and of the audience; police torture, if we get near enough to an adequate representation of it, cannot be used in this way.

That there should be something nasty at the centre of *Tosca* is the result of Puccini's method when it goes beyond the bounds of what it can handle. The method is a special and very effective invention, and it has a powerful appeal which is rooted in the traditions of Italian opera, and indeed in the basic experience of its performance. But the method cannot deal with a genuinely threatening content, and when it fails, the spectator's revulsion is considerable, for he feels himself not only exploited, but an accomplice in his own exploitation. *Tosca* is remarkable in providing some of the most striking achievements of Puccini's artifice, and also the most unnerving display of its limitations.

Note

1. 'Notes on Music and Opera', in *The Dyer's Hand* (London, 1963), pp. 468–9. Auden agreed, however, that opera can be the ideal vehicle of 'tragic myth'. See also 'The World of Opera', in his *Secondary Worlds* (London, 1969).

12

Comments on *Opera and Ideas: From Mozart to Strauss* by Paul Robinson

There are a lot of points that I should have liked to take up in Paul Robinson's very interesting book, which I admire because it extends to opera a serious level of intellectual interest that is taken for granted as appropriate in other dramatic arts but is rarely applied to opera; and also because, even more unusually, it obeys the precept that if you want to understand opera you must trust its music. However, because of the limitations of time, my remarks will be mostly about Wagner and Strauss, and in particular Wagner.

The work of Wagner's that Robinson considers in his book is *Die Meistersinger*, and he puts it in comparison with *Der Rosenkavalier*. By a technique rather similar to that which he applies to *The Marriage of Figaro* and *The Barber of Seville*, he takes two works that have something in common (in each case, one work greater than the other) and elicits some differences that he associates with differences in their historical circumstances. In considering opera and ideas, Robinson has in mind throughout opera and the history of ideas.

The resemblance that Robinson finds between the Wagner and Strauss works is of course different from that between Mozart's and Rossini's operas; the latter share an author as literary source, the former pair share a structure in their plot, a structure of renunciation. But there is surely another difference, which affects the comparison. Rossini must have known *The Marriage of Figaro*, and that knowledge affected his work in general, but, as Robinson's account brings out, it had little distinctive effect on the *Barber*; while Strauss has *Meistersinger* in mind, as he has Wagner always in mind. This is just one way in which *Rosenkavalier* is immensely historically and stylistically self-conscious, and there are many others, such as the way in which it refers, as has often been remarked, to three different historical periods. There is the time of the action, taken up at least once into the music; the time of the Baron's waltzes; and the time of the work itself, which – as Robinson rightly says – is rather ambivalently revealed in a lot of its music. All this is replicated in the text, which combines elaborately archaic forms of address with pieces of knowing Viennese reflection hardly available to an eighteenth-century Feldmarschallin.

As Robinson notes, Strauss tries to turn this machinery in the scene of the presentation of the rose to the expression of simple and naïve goodness and love (as he does in the duet at the end of the opera, a cynical and unsuccessful attempt to borrow innocence from *The Magic Flute*). Beautiful as it is, I do not myself find this as successful as Robinson does. It fails in the same way as Jokanaan's music in *Salome*, i.e. it is kitsch. The failure is a lot less drastic, because *Rosenkavalier* is all, to some degree, kitsch. I don't go as far as Joseph Kerman's judgment that the rose scene 'has all the solidity of a fifty-cent valentine'; Kerman is a puritan who detests kitsch on principle. But if it is regarded as expressive rather than decorative, there is something false about it, because the manifest conditions of its production conflict with what is being expressed.

The point of this is that the vast self-consciousness of *Rosenkavalier* – its exploitation, sometimes engaging, sometimes boring, sometimes disgusting, of its own historical situation – means that it is already quite different from any work of Wagner, above all *Meistersinger*. That is indeed a difference between 1911 and the 1860s. (It is a difference paralleled in that between Verdi and Puccini, except that Strauss can, above all in *Rosenkavalier*, be seen, if you like, not just as someone who rejected modernism but as a postmodernist *avant la lettre*, whereas Puccini can't.) The great historical self-consciousness of so much twentieth-century art of course itself puts questions to the history of ideas. But it is this, very general, difference, I think, that overwhelmingly contributes to the contrast between these works (even if we grant, with Isaiah Berlin, that Wagner himself, in contrast to Verdi, belongs to the 'sentimental' or self-conscious type of artist, rather than the 'naïve').

When we take this very general difference into account, we have less reason, I think, to insist on the difference of content that Robinson picks out and tries to explain historically, namely that *Meistersinger* is social and *Rosenkavalier* purely psychological. Society is not denied in the latter; it is merely taken for granted, like hundreds of other things in so knowing a work. In a passage from the libretto that Robinson himself quotes, the remarks of members of society are themselves an important element in the Marschallin's fear of the passage of time.

What is true is that *Meistersinger*, as against *Rosenkavalier*, is not just social but political. In the regrettable passage about German art (which Cosima made Wagner put in against his better judgment) it is indeed explicitly political. At the beginning of his book, Robinson says that he has chosen to consider *Meistersinger* partly because other works of Wagner are too consciously and explicitly related to ideas to bring out the kind of influence or association he wants to illustrate. There is a difference between *Meistersinger* and Wagner's other mature works in some such respect, but I do not think this gets it right. The difference is that the text is less abstract and less explicitly philosophical than, manifestly, that of *Tristan* or most of the *Ring* or – though it again is rather different – *Parsifal*; but this is because the ideas are more directly and unambiguously expressed in the action, which in turn is more locally and concretely political.

Meistersinger is no less a political drama than *An Enemy of the People*, but it is a lot more as well. Robinson has put it the other way round, by making it a psychological story of renunciation with a social setting, but I think this centres Sachs's renunciation too much (the reference to King Mark in *Tristan* at the critical moment in Act III, which Robinson mentions, is in fact deployed, both in words and music, with some wry irony). Sachs is its hero, but it is essential that it isn't named for him.

Now I would not say that *Meistersinger* is Wagner's most political work – but I think that Robinson should. For he says that Verdi's work is more political than that of Wagner, on the grounds that Verdi often puts before us historically located men of power, while Wagner's works, with the exception of *Meistersinger* (and, I suppose one should add, *Rienzi*), are mostly placed in vaguely medieval or mythological settings. And in this sense *Meistersinger* is closer to a particular political reality than the others. But I wouldn't accept this level of the identification of the political. It seems to me obvious that the most political of Wagner's works is the *Ring*, even though it is determinedly unlocated in history. In order to agree with this one doesn't have to accept Shaw's or some similar reading of it as an allegorical critique of capitalism. Those elements surely exist in it, as Chéreau's wonderful centennial production of it – unlike many other such attempts – brought out (not only in its many successes but also in

an obvious mistake, that the yet undisturbed Rhinemaidens at the beginning of *Rheingold* should have been represented as already involved in the
industrial complex). The *Ring* is basically political just because it is
concerned in manifold ways with the exercise of power, its possibilities,
limitations, necessities and costs.

So, of course, as Robinson well brings out, is *Don Carlos*, and it might
have been interesting if Robinson had brought his comparative method
to bear on King Philip and Wotan. But even in that great work, Verdi
subordinates matters intrinsic to the exercise of power to the human,
psychological and ethical interest of the characters involved in it, whereas
Wagner, in the *Ring*, deploys an action that is structured in part by the
long-range concerns and consequences of power, reaching often beyond
the consciousness of particular characters. Wotan is unique in the degree
to which these facts, and the associated responsibilities, are represented
in his consciousness, alongside more ordinary – one might have said,
everyday – concerns.

In fact, Wagner runs extreme risks, both in *Rheingold* and in *Walküre*, in
putting together these levels of concern. It has been said that the *Ring*
under its world-historical trappings is often only a bourgeois domestic
drama, and this criticism, if true, would be deeply damaging; unlike the
perfectly correct, and non-damaging, description of *Aida* as a chamber
opera with processions. The criticism is false, and the ways in which
Wagner holds it at bay would make a revealing study of his skill. He
himself said that his art was that of transition, and the musical devices that
embody this art are what enable him to move convincingly from domestic
to historical or metaphysical preoccupations: one example is the
wonderful passage in *Walküre* in which Fricka finally defeats Wotan in
their closely argued quarrel over whether Siegmund is to be defended:
'Deiner ew'gen Gattin heilige Ehre' ('The sacred honour of your eternal
wife').

Wagner's many critics, those who hate and in some cases, it must be
said, fear his art, will cite just this kind of thing as an instance of his powers
as a theatrical showman, a trickster, old Klingsor, as Debussy called him,
the original inventor (to borrow a title of Angela Carter's) of the infernal
desire machines of Dr Hoffmann. But it is hard to sustain this, I think, if
one looks carefully at the way in which the junctions between these
various concerns are not just concealed by the music but expressed by it,
and also represented in the consciousness of, above all, Wotan himself.

Robinson's contrast of *Meistersinger* with *Rosenkavalier* as social to psychological is confined to those two works and is not, I think, supposed to carry over into any larger comparison of the two composers. But inasmuch as he connects this with a change in general consciousness between two historical periods, one would expect it to be more generally revealed. In that light, there is really a problem, since *Tristan*, written just before *Meistersinger*, must surely be one of the most intensely solitary, inwards-turned, unsocial, depth-psychological works ever written. This raises, in fact, a general problem about Robinson's method: if the difference between two works is to be explained in any way in terms of a more general difference between two periods, then the difference has to extend beyond the two works under comparison. A historical difference might of course be focused more narrowly by its being the case that it shows itself in the way in which *a given subject* is handled at different periods, and I think that is what Robinson has in mind; but then it becomes all the more crucial to identify what the given subject is. It may be that Wagner could have written a more purely psychological version of the story of Hans Sachs if he had wanted to, but was writing something else. One piece of evidence that he could have written a purely psychological drama of that kind is *Tristan*.

In fact, even *Tristan* has a social dimension, a world outside Tristan and Isolde, but it is exclusively located in relation to them. It plays a part in a more general feature of the work, the way in which its three acts relate differently to time. Each act starts with music off-stage, which provides the basis for the opening musical development. The dramatic content of that music establishes for each act a different relation to time. At the beginning of the first act, the sailor's song, drifting down from high up the mast, looks forward. The constant sense of that approaching future holds the act together.

The hunting horns with which the second act begins relate to the present and to what, they pretend, is happening elsewhere. They tell us, as do Brangäne's warnings, of something Tristan's and Isolde's music denies, that they are surrounded at that very moment by a world of social and personal relations.

In the third act, we have Tristan without Isolde, and it becomes finally his drama. It, too, starts with off-stage music, and this relates to the past. But it is essential to the power of this work that Tristan cannot be allowed simply to expire on Melot's sword; he has to pass through knowledge, and his recovery of that is the subject of his great monologue, the climax of the work. That is, above all, why *Tristan,* though its libretto is more textured by vaguely philosophical ideas than any other of Wagner's works, is a psychological work rather than a metaphysical one, and is in fact a drama.

I feel that these points about *Tristan* and the character of the *Ring* as a political drama both give the same lesson, that the ideas to which a Wagnerian opera, at least, gives expression have to be understood at a level that lies not just below the libretto but below the libretto as musically presented at particular moments. *Tristan* is a psychological drama and not a metaphysical meditation; moreover, it is not a drama of a triangle, of trust and betrayal, but a drama of the self in time, about the loss of self in passion and the recovery of self in memory. The *Ring* is a political drama not in a way that excludes the psychological; its whole aim is to integrate the two (there is an eventual failure of that integration, but that is not the work's failure, it is the failure that it represents). And in each case these features of the work come out only in the experience of it as a musical whole.

I do very much agree with Robinson that the power of opera particularly lies at the intersection of the social and psychological worlds, and in its capacity to express both at once. As he also says, the way in which ideas are expressed in opera is likely to relate particularly to the images they bear of the self, its relations to others, society, time and its own history. But, as I am sure he would agree, the exploration of these matters can be carried to further levels, which go still deeper in the right direction, that is to say, into the music.

A last point: with respect to that exploration, I find it odd that he would say, at the end of his book, that the idea of a positivist opera is almost a contradiction in terms. Of course it is true, if it means an opera that declares positivism; but – whatever people say about Wagner and the philosophy of Schopenhauer – that's true of any opera and any philosophy. What is in question is whether any opera could express and mobilise for its dramatic purposes a picture of the self and of human life that bore a revealing relation to the picture of those things given or implied by positivism. I cannot argue it here, but there surely is such an opera – in fact two, the two greatest operas of the twentieth century, *Wozzeck* and *Lulu.*

13

The Marriage and the Flute
Tippett and Mozart

In an essay written in 1944 called 'Contracting into Abundance', Michael Tippett spoke of 'the fact of divided man' and the ideal of 'the whole man', and went on to say (as he put it later) that 'the most enchanting expression of a general state where theological man is balanced against natural man is Mozart's *Magic Flute*'. A pattern drawn from *The Magic Flute* was in Tippett's mind from the beginning of the generation of *The Midsummer Marriage*, and while he was convinced that 'no-one now can match the innocence, tenderness and simplicity with which that mythological experience was presented', the exemplar remained with him in fashioning this, his first opera: an opera which is a comedy, with a rather special version of what he saw as the one and only comic plot, the unexpected hindrances to an eventual marriage.

But does the plot of the intriguing and very beautiful opera that Tippett achieved really resemble that of *The Magic Flute*? How do the resemblances, such as they are, help us to understand *The Midsummer Marriage*? In some respects, very obviously, the operas are alike. In both works there are two couples, one more spiritual, or called to higher things, than the other. In both operas, again, humans encounter some version of the supernatural, and in both, the other realm and its powers are expressed in symbols that do not belong to any orthodox religion. In *The Magic Flute* the machinery is masonic, vaguely Egyptian and at the limit sheer pantomime; the prince Tamino, its hero, is 'japonisch' – not so much Japanese (as William Mann has put it) as Ruritanian. *The Midsummer Marriage* is set in the modern world, has a priest and priestess in a Greek temple, and its Celtic hero and heroine undergo a Hindu transfiguration in the third act.

In both the operas, moreover, underlying the assorted symbols and doing something to unite them, is a meaning which the work tacitly claims as universal. For Mozart and his rather distracted librettist Schikaneder it was the message of Reason, Nature and Wisdom, the words that are inscribed on the three temples which Tamino encounters when he enters Sarastro's realm. In Tippett's text there is a symbolic structure with strong Jungian associations, expressed in the many binary oppositions that are invoked (between the sexes, for instance) and in the references to the four elements, the four seasons and the various beasts that all figure in the Ritual Dances.

Once one reaches these universal currents that flow through the two works, however, one begins to see that the resemblances between them may not go very deep. Tippett's opera is in fact more involved than Mozart's in the 'supernatural', in the sense at least of significances that transcend familiar human understandings. In his book *Moving into Aquarius*, Tippett refers several times to Stefan George's line 'ich fühle Luft von anderen Planeten', 'I feel the air from other planets', and a powerful charge is given to *The Midsummer Marriage* by the sense that Mark and Jenifer are involved in, and the other characters are encountering, an order of things beyond ordinary calculation.

Mozart's characters are certainly in a strange enough world, but it is notable how, under the level of the magic tricks, there is a robust commitment to the everyday powers of humanity and to a belief that human benevolence and practical good sense can prevail. There is a significant glimpse of this (in a particularly masonic form, perhaps) when Tamino, approaching the temples, remarks on their workmanship: 'these columns prove that skill, art, industry reside here; where action rules and idleness is banished, vice cannot easily gain control'. These temples have been designed – they are the product of thought and work; they are not magical emanations or (like the temple of Tippett's Ancients) unspecifically mysterious ruins. Indeed, the message of *The Magic Flute* is that this life, our life, can be made to embody the aspirations expressed in religion. The last words of Act I, repeated by the three boys at the beginning of the finale of Act II, express this in the noblest tones of the late eighteenth century: when virtue prevails, when peace fills the hearts of men, 'dann ist die Erd ein Himmelreich, und Sterbliche den Göttern gleich' – 'the earth becomes a heavenly kingdom, and mortals are like gods'.

An unquestioned acceptance of such values unites Tamino and Pamina, as it eventually unites them both with the world of Sarastro. The relations of Mark and Jenifer in *The Midsummer Marriage*, and the relations of both of them to reason and truth, are more complex. Mark, first of all, is already, to some obscure extent, part of the supernatural world. He is 'a young man of unknown parentage', who has seen the Ancients 'since boyhood'. He already knows the name of the dancer, Strephon. Yet it is Jenifer, in flight from her bullying father King Fisher, who is drawn to explore this world and precipitates the division of their paths that occurs in Act I. It is she who says, 'It isn't love I want, but truth', and says it again when he responds only with the adoring, and also self-adoring, lyricism of 'The summer morning dances in my heart'. She may seem to echo Pamina, who, asked by Papageno what they can say to Sarastro, in a phrase of famous beauty and confidence sings, 'die Wahrheit' – 'the truth'. But the echo is a false one, and significantly so: in Pamina's world there is no conflict between love and truth, and there is no conflict between her and her loved one (except for the moment when, later, she thinks he does not love her).

Jenifer, on the other hand, needs to 'thrust her lover from her' before she can marry him. She has first to make a journey which will free her from external attachments. Her departure has the effect of setting Mark off on his own journey, one that in the first instance sends him to a place of darkness and need, in order that (as I read it) he can separate his joy in Jenifer from his pleasure in himself. This progress does serve to separate him from his exultant ego, but at the same time it identifies him more urgently with physical desire, with the rhythms of 'stallions stamping' that the chorus of men take up from him in the Act I finale.

When Jenifer comes back, she also is detached from the ego, particularly from her aim of marrying in order to get away from her father; but in coming to this she has moved too far beyond the world of desire and has reached a state of spiritual purity and calm which leaves out physical need altogether. (King Fisher's intervention at this point – 'We live on earth and not in heaven, nor is there disgrace in that' – is true and also entirely misses the point.) Now it is necessary that each of them should go in the other direction and accomplish the compensating change that will make each a whole person and their marriage a whole marriage.

That second departure occurs at the end of Act I. In Act II Mark and Jenifer do not appear at all, and it is only in the finale of the opera, after the fourth Ritual Dance, that they reappear, transfigured and united, in a Hindu hieratic pose. By now there is no further question of what in psychological terms has happened to them. The unity of each, and their uniting with each other, is displayed and not explained. It occurs as an outcome and a celebration, and not as part of the action.

After their first conflict, the action of *The Midsummer Marriage*, both dramatic and psychological, has in fact very little to do with Mark and Jenifer. What the chorus calls, at the end of Act I, 'the perils of the royal way' are not enacted for us. Almost everything that visibly happens does so to the more earthbound pair of Bella and Jack, and when they grow, as to some extent they do, it is in ways that are directly involved in the action. They are not at any serious level parallel to Papageno and Papagena in *The Magic Flute*. It is only with respect to their future, their life after the opera is over, that we are invited to see them as similar, and Tippett's suggestion of this is explicit in the passage in Act II where Bella and Jack look forward to the arrival of 'a little Jack or a little Bella'. Though the setting of this 1950s suburban dream is very appealing, its content may seem dated now; more generally Bella and Jack, and King Fisher as well, share stereotyped assumptions about men's and women's roles, and it seems that this may be intended as a sign of their attachment to the everyday order of things, since with Mark and Jenifer it is not the same. In their world, contrasts are indeed drawn between male and female principles but they are seen as forces within one person, whichever their sex.

In fact we are shown in a brief but important moment in Act III that Jack and Bella themselves grow in these respects. When they crucially defy King Fisher and precipitate the climax of the action, they do so together, and it is Bella who takes the lead: 'Ah, Jack! our moment's at its height.' This is their last appearance in the opera, and when they leave and the chorus sings for them, 'He must leap and she must fall, when the bright sun shines on midsummer-day', we have the sense that their life has already become a different order of enterprise than we would have gathered from their domestic dream and from all the earlier emphasis on his spanners and her hair-do.

Perhaps the most significant comparison between *The Magic Flute* and *The Midsummer Marriage* lies not so much in their plots or characters or symbolism as in their relations to the operatic tradition, in the kind of opera each is. Pierre Boulez has said about *Parsifal*, in his remarkable essay 'Approaches to *Parsifal*' (1970); reprinted in *Orientations* (London, 1986), that it was the culmination in its time of a tradition going back to Schütz and Monteverdi, a synthesis between the Passions and the Opera, between a representation that is abstract and imaginary and one that is concrete and theatrical. Though Boulez places *The Magic Flute*, naturally enough, among the concrete and theatrical, he has good reason to mention it in this connection: the role of the chorus and of Sarastro can be understood in terms of this tradition, not adding to the enacted events so much as placing them in a more comprehensive setting.

In these terms, *The Midsummer Marriage* is a very special kind of opera, one that constructs a space for itself not only between operatic drama and oratorio but between both of these and masque. In such a work it is particularly important that not everything that happens occurs in the succession of action: we are told a good deal more than the story. It is appropriate that a section which contains some of the work's finest music, Sosostris's *scena* in Act III, is in its content and tone much more than anything required in terms of the plot. At this point, it is as though the enacted events of the opera have become only a small part, the most immediately active part, of a larger whole, which is expressed in the orchestra and in a voice which is not that of a character but reaches beyond the characters.

If this is so, then it is also what makes possible a surprising musical effect: that at the noble climax of this solo – 'You who consult me, should never doubt me. Clean let the heart be, of each seeker' – we should hear as entirely appropriate an echo of Elgar. Among the many resources of English music on which Tippett draws, he can find a place – just because he is writing an opera which presents more than its story – for the voice of a composer whose great dramatic powers never found expression in opera.

14

Janáček's Modernism

Doing Less with More in Music and Philosophy

This essay was written for a volume celebrating the seventieth birthday of the composer Alexander Goehr.

Milan Kundera has written, 'I see the art of ellipses as crucial. It insists that we go directly to the heart of things. In that regard, I am reminded of the composer I've admired passionately since I was a child, Leoš Janáček.' Kundera emphasised particularly Janáček's methods of leaving out the 'superfluous notes': the transitions, the decorations, the bits that merely fill in. Hence his harsh juxtapositions and the bare repetitions. Kundera also said that Janáček created a new world for opera, 'a world of prose'; he was interested above all in the analogies to Janáček's music that he might create in the old world of prose, in his own writing.

Sandy Goehr and I have often talked about the demands of modernism – the case, above all and unsurprisingly, of the composer who still acknowledges those demands but does not necessarily interpret them in terms of a specific set of techniques, those of the Second Viennese School. We have talked, too, about the analogies, such as they may be, between those aims in music and the aims of certain kinds of writing, in particular the kind of writing I myself do, which is philosophy. I do not recall Sandy's saying very much about Janáček, but when I saw these remarks of Kundera's, quoted by Vanda Prochazka in his essay on *Kát'a Kabanová* in the Glyndebourne programme book (2002), they brought back vividly to me the concerns of those conversations.

There is no need to suppose that Janáček's operas are among the very greatest: there are others (though not many modern ones) that are more complex musically, dramatically and psychologically. In particular, the sacrifice of musical development carries a substantial cost. But in his finest works he found forms of expression that, for me at any rate, have a quite specially direct and disarming effect. He found at crucial moments an absolutely honest lyricism, not kitschy or contrived, which is an unquestionably convincing extension of the 'prose' that is carried by his constant attention to the rhythms of speech. The closing scene of the *Vixen* is one example, and another, particularly striking, case is in the last act of *The Makropulos Case*, when after a lot of argumentative exchanges Emilia Marty renounces the formula that keeps her alive: Janáček very slightly opens out the material that up to then has been kept under tight control, and it is as though the roof has fallen in.

It is (of course) a matter of doing more with less – in contrast, to take an easy one, to the overloaded and (at least after *Elektra*) relentlessly ingratiating structures of Strauss. It was always a demand of modernism to do more with less, as it was to avoid at once the flabby and the kitschy. But those demands always bring a question with them: *what* more is done with less of *what*? That is still the question when one turns to the case of philosophy.

In some modernist philosophers there is an analogy to Janáček's ellipses, the elimination of transitions: with them, juxtaposition and repetition provide the structure. But it is not clear how well this can work, indeed how well it does work even in the greatest of such philosophers, Wittgenstein. The problem perhaps lies in this, that even if the loss of large-scale development in Janáček is counted a loss, the result is unquestionably music, and very powerfully so; but philosophy without argumentative development, philosophy in which all the *therefore's* have been replaced by *and's* or by spaces, is dubiously philosophy at all. Or rather, if it is philosophy, as Wittgenstein's quite certainly is, it is so because it is about earlier philosophy, even if it does not say so: in his case, the earlier philosophy was often his own. That other aspect of modernism, historical self-consciousness, has to sustain the identity of the enterprise altogether. This is not just a classificatory or organisational problem, as to what is to be labelled 'philosophy'. It is a deeper question of philosophy's claim on anyone's attention. Janác̆ek's music does not have to prove to anyone that it is worth someone's attention – it commands it. But philosophers do not usually have much to make anyone interested in them except their arguments.

Modern philosophy has one sure modernist credential in its rejection of kitsch. In its technical complexity and a certain rhetoric of formalism it can rightly contrast itself with writing that cheaply passes as philosophy, with its false comforts or bogus profundities or self-satisfied and costless gestures of despair. Avoiding such things is not a particularly modern aim – it is something that philosophy has had to do from its earliest days in ancient Greece. There has been, rather, a characteristically modernist turn of the screw in an extended suspicion of what counts as hollow in these ways. But the basic modernist demand of doing more with less is not met simply by formalism and technicality and the rejection of the merely edifying. That can result merely in doing less with more: the 'rattle of machinery', as an old and bad-tempered colleague of mine in the University of London used to call it, takes over once more, and the only difference is that now the rattle is clearly that of machinery. What has to be done with less is – at the end of the line or, better, at the end of some lines – to speak truthfully to a real human concern, to something that could disturb or interest a grown-up person quite apart from any involvement in professional philosophy.

Of course no intellectual construction, in philosophy or in the arts, speaks to anyone in a way that is not mediated by some history and some set of expectations, and it is a mark of modernism not only to accept that fact but in certain ways to exploit it. Unselfconscious modernism is a contradiction in terms. It is an extraordinary achievement of Janáček's to have used a very original modernist technique to cut through its own peculiarities and to produce something that is experienced as an exceptionally direct address to very powerful feelings. A philosopher will understand, ruefully enough, that no philosophical words can ever do what music can do, in this as in many other respects. Yet Janáček can stand as a reminder even to a philosopher of what should be done: granted essential technical complexity and inescapable self-consciousness, to address, express and restructure real emotions in ways that neither evade them with formalism nor degrade them into kitsch.

15

Authenticity and Re-creation

Musicology, Performance and Production

Edited version of a lecture given to the International Musicological Society

To love music, as I do – or rather, I should say, to love quite a lot of music, since there is a lot I do not know, some I am indifferent to, and some, as there is for any sensible person who cares about it, that I hate – this does not mean that even in an amateurish way one grasps much of the musicologist's crafts. The converse, too, is at least conceivable – that mastery of the musicological crafts does not necessarily imply a love of music.

But when I try to imagine what this might be like, I find it is quite hard – partly because, if you have ever liked music, it is hard to imagine what it is to dislike it. But it is also because there is a difference in the musicologist's case from all the others, that almost everybody who studies music can, to some degree and in some form or another, play it, and that gives immediate encouragement and hope.

This relation between the study and the performance of music parallels, of course, the original relation that exists in music between performance and creation. Music is virtually unique in this respect. For many arts, there is no performance. Where there is performance, the creator and the performer are rarely the same person, and where they are the same person (as they sometimes are in the theatre, for instance) the two roles are usually related in a merely extrinsic way. This may be so even in what may seem a quite favourable case, such as Noël Coward appearing in his own plays. With music, the relationship is, or at least has been, very much deeper than this. Not all composers, of course, are quite at Liszt's end of the spectrum, where composition can seem an overflow of performance. In the case of orchestral composition, there are many degrees of performance expertise that can underlie the ability to write for various instruments, from Elgar at one end to Berlioz, who, I understand, could not play many instruments very well, and in particular had not been taught the piano: as my French dictionary of music elegantly puts it, 'son père s'étant méfié du trop grand pouvoir qu'aurait pu exercer le piano sur l'enfant'.

There are, of course, the standard reactionary horror stories about contemporary composers who cannot play anything, including their own works – indeed, in the more extreme stories, cannot recognise their own works when played; but those stories are, as we know, typically told by cynical orchestral musicians or, just occasionally, by less successful conservative composers. But when all allowances and qualifications have been made, there has been a traditional connection between composing and playing, just as there is an intimate connection between performance and the mere existence of music.

If that is right, then perhaps we can take another step: the scholarship of music is intimately involved with the scholarship of the performance of music. I know that not all musicology is related even indirectly to performance or to the history of performance. Still, it must be important that there is a special relation to performance. This is why musicology even at its most austerely textual could not be just like textual criticism. Indeed, there are more problems about what textual criticism is in purely literary studies than textual critics have always been willing to admit, but whatever such a critic may be doing to the text of Propertius or – perhaps this is more immediately to the point – Sophocles, he or she is not preparing it for performance. Where words are concerned, the preparation of a text always underdetermines performance. Of course in the case of music a score also underdetermines performance, which is why there are interestingly different performances and interpretations, but the musicological preparation of a score always anticipates performance intellectually, if not in the practical sense that it has a particular performance in view. It is at any rate deeply involved in questions of performance style.

This is never so in the literary case. There can be cases in which historical research determines to an unusual degree what happens on a stage – I assume this is what is happening at the new Globe Theatre in London. But, first, the Globe effect, as we may call it, is incomplete – though I have not been there, I take it that the pronunciation is not usually authentically Elizabethan. Moreover, even the most enthusiastic supporters of the Globe recognise that this way of doing Shakespeare is one option among others.

No-one supposes that this type of performance – or a yet more authentically Elizabethanly pronounced version of it – is what it is to perform *Henry V*, that this is what *Henry V* is. Yet with some music at least, it does seem that the aim of historical scholarship is to establish what a given work is, in the sense of determining pretty closely what a performance would be that was a performance of this work.

Of course this does not apply to the scenic and other non-musical aspects of opera, and no-one expects it to do so. If one did aim at a performance of *Beatrice di Tenda*, for example, which was to the greatest possible degree determined by historical research, everyone would know that it was, like the Globe effect, a special option. I suggest that there is a real asymmetry here between music and literary works, even those, notably drama, that aim at performance. This corresponds to two different conceptions of authenticity. It inevitably follows from these differences that in the case of opera, where both the contrasting elements are involved, the two conceptions of authenticity converge on it, as one might say, from different directions.

It is a significant fact that we have seen in the opera house in recent years the coexistence of two kinds of radicalism: an increasing 'authenticity' of orchestral and vocal performance, based on historical research; and productions and sets that display all degrees of rethinking and creativity up to the now notorious extremes of directorial whimsy – which themselves are more or less what have come to be expected. In abstract terms, these two developments might seem to go in opposite directions. It is true, of course, that they can conflict, as when the production makes it impossible for the singers to express what the music requires or invites them to express. (This is not a conflict between music and drama: it is a conflict between the dramatic contribution of the music and the dramatic contribution of the stage.) But this is a matter of particular failures, not of what is intrinsic to the two kinds of radicalism. Put together in the right way, quite extreme versions of the two kinds of radicalism can produce a triumphant success: a notable example has been Peter Sellars's Glyndebourne production of *Theodora*. What is significant in this is that the two kinds of radicalism combine to the same end – an uncluttered, seemingly transparent enactment of what this particular work is.

I mentioned two conceptions of authenticity, roughly one appropriate to music and one to dramatic text: let us call them the authenticity of veracity and the authenticity of re-creation. Music drama requires, or at least can sustain, both, and in a successful example they come together. In the case of *Theodora*, the musical performance offers (or so I suppose) a closer approximation to what were, precisely, Handel's means of expression. The production offers a version of what this drama, these emotional relations, can mean in terms that make sense to us, now. It finds visual and dramatic equivalences, which work for us, to the expressive content both of the words, and of the music as that music, partly with the help of musicological scholarship, is now presented to us. But no presentation of what happens on the stage that was itself determined by historical research could have a comparable effect, except, very occasionally, by luck.

In fact, the idea of a dramatic production, for instance of an opera, that was 'authentic' in the sense in which musical performances can aim to be 'authentic' (something we shall come back to) – that is to say, a production which aimed exclusively at the authenticity of veracity – seems to be virtually nonsensical. Critics nostalgically refer to what they call a 'traditional' production. But they cannot mean we should be given what Wagner in 1876 in Bayreuth actually had – for one thing, we know what Wagner thought of what he got in 1876. Could we say, what Wagner would have liked in 1876? That is an altogether indeterminate conception, above all in the case of this particular artist, since Wagner's wants in this as in most other respects were *grenzenlos* (boundless). Moreover, since Wagner was not content with the resources he had, and since in any case the question is one for us, of what we should do, even the most devoted intentionalist has to ask, not what Wagner wanted granted the resources he had, but what he would have wanted if he had had our resources. What are 'our resources'? That must mean, among other things, the resources we need to present his works to audiences who have seen what we have seen – and seen, not only on the stage. We are back, unsurprisingly, where we started, with the problems of staging Wagner's works for us, now.

I have put this in terms of the artist's desires or wishes, but I am not suggesting that such ideas are essential to the notion of authenticity. It is particularly tempting to move in this direction when pursuing such questions in the case of Wagner, just because he was an exceptionally devoted and prolix expositor of his own objectives. The point I am stressing is that even if one tries to think in terms of the composer's desires and wishes, as one may be encouraged to do in this relatively favourable case, one still ends up where one started. It underlies the point that at least when one is dealing with the case of drama, there is simply no alternative to what I have called the authenticity of re-creation.

We reached that conclusion in this case by a process of what seems to me, at least, the merest common sense. However, once we have got there, we may reasonably wonder what is going to happen to the idea of authenticity more generally, in particular to the idea of the authenticity of veracity which I applied to musical performances. I have so far taken this idea for granted: as I put it in the case of *Theodora*, 'the musical performance offers a closer approximation to what were, precisely, Handel's means of expression'. This does not say 'Handel's intentions'. There is of course a large general subject here in the philosophy of the arts, one which must be of concern to the more philosophical parts of musicology. If the situation is anything like that in the philosophy of the other arts, the question is not so much whether the artist's intentions matter to understanding the work, but rather what counts relevantly as an artistic intention. In the case of other arts, people who oppose the idea that understanding a work involves recovering the artist's intentions often base their opposition on stupid ideas of what, in general, an intention is. They speak as though the intentional significance of an action, any action, is to be thought of as something written in a balloon coming out of the agent's head, rather than figured in the action itself. (In much the same way, many post-structuralist rejections of the 'authorial self' are directed against conceptions of the self that owe much more to Platonic or Cartesian philosophy than to any everyday workable conception of a person.)

The concerns of musicology, I take it, will not often be concentrated on external or anecdotal declarations of compositorial intentions, though they no doubt sometimes come into it. The question must rather be what the musical resources of a given time made possible, including what extensions of those resources were possible, and these are in the first place historical and interpretative questions. It must, I assume, be an aim of musicological scholarship to show us what artistic aims at a given time for a given composer or group of composers were even possible. This applies to the question of what expressive intentions, in the sense of musical intentions, were possible, but it must reach into other relevant questions as well. If, rather naïvely, we think of an authentic performance as a performance of a work which the composer would have recognised and approved as a performance of that work, it will matter what ideas the composer had or could have had of another performance of that very work – what idea, for instance, he might have had of a performance of that very work by different forces. What ideas may have been available at a given time and place I take to be a matter of history, one sort of history that musicologists do.

There are many related ideas that are equally the concern of such history: the notion, for instance, of what the composer can reasonably be thought to have wanted. This is not the notion of what as a matter of fact he expected, since he often had good reason to expect the worst, but what he would have wanted if he had known it was possible. The problems and indeterminacies lurking in this line of thought are obviously much better known to musicologists than to me, and I am not rash enough even to start asking about the exact differences there are between various cases, and what these differences mean for the notion of authenticity. There is the case of something that many eighteenth-century composers presumably wanted and rarely got, an orchestra which could play in tune; that is a case, certainly, where we are happy to give them some version of what they wanted. How far do we go from that before we get to the desire that some have ascribed to Beethoven in his later years, to have something more like a modern piano?

This is one range of problems that bears on what I called earlier the authenticity of veracity. There is another, and quite different problem – one that is even more general, and in fact ubiquitous. We who now hear musical works from the past have heard many things that the composer and the original audiences had not heard, and our expectations and ranges of comparison are quite different. This sets an *a priori* limit on the idea of authenticity. If you generated exactly the same sound waves as were brought about in seventeenth-century Mantua or eighteenth-century Leipzig, you would not make the same music, since no-one has seventeenth- or eighteenth-century ears. Everyone knows this, and it looks fatal to at least a naïve theory of the authenticity of veracity. Yet, curiously, this very general and seemingly fatal objection does not seem to matter much for the practice of music. It does not matter for the practice, I think, because every successful move in the 'authentic' direction itself helps to re-educate people's ears. It does not re-educate them to what they would have been in earlier times, an idea which I take to be meaningless. Rather, they are re-educated so that they can hear these works for the first time. When performance decisions guided by ideals of authenticity are good decisions, as they often are, it is not because they make the music sound old but because they make it sound new.

I once heard a performance of the Bach B minor Mass given by the Freiburger Barockorchester and a choir associated with them (directed by Thomas Hengelbrock). I do not know exactly how 'authentic' it was. There was a small orchestra; a choir of about thirty; the soloists were part of the choir; there were male altos; some of the instruments were clearly more 'original' than others. It may be that, taken altogether, it bore a closer relation to something that took place (or perhaps took place) in 1749 than most performances in the meantime that have claimed to be of this work. It was still a long way away from any such event in 1749: starting with the fact that it happened in the Kammermusiksaal of the Berlin Philharmonie, not much like the architectural, religious or social context of any event in 1749. What made it quite wonderful was certainly something that was a creation of 1997.

I think that what is suggested by such examples and by these lines of thought is that all authenticity is, in the end, the authenticity of re-creation, but that in the case of music – and, I suspect, uniquely in the case of music – there is a particular kind of re-creation that is specially guided by an ideal of authenticity as veracity. Musicological scholarship is essentially involved in that enterprise, though, obviously, some areas of it are further away from that enterprise than others. Some musicological research, I take it, is simply history which is directed to music, and it is like other kinds of history, though it needs a knowledge of music to do it: dating an autograph, finding out when Monteverdi went to Venice. But there will be no sharp lines to separate history and, eventually, re-creation. There is the rich historical activity of establishing what expressive means were available, what significance particular means had in relation to others, what modes of decorum or propriety made sense, what violations of them were intelligible as expressive violations and not simply blunders. Knowing these things helps us not only to understand, but to re-create, because they suggest ways in which we can construct analogues and correspondences to those means of expression, not by making the same sounds, but by making sounds which are indeed to an important degree like the sounds of an earlier time and which have a similar expressive significance for us – where the idea of 'a similar significance' is itself formed in the course of such enquiries.

Besides the problems of the authenticity of veracity, musicology is also inevitably involved in what is directly and immediately the authenticity of re-creation, the kind that is involved in performing dramatic texts. In the nature of the case, this applies in the first instance to opera, but it has wider implications as well. As I said in the case of Wagner, the problem is set by the fact that the works are being presented to people, namely us, who have seen many things that the composer and his original audience had not seen, and not only on the stage. It is analogous to the problems set by the fact that we have heard other music, but it is much more radical, and in this case, I have already suggested, there is no ideal of veracity to assist our re-creation.

The problem becomes still more radical when the issues raised are ethical, political and, in the broadest sense, ideological; and it is most radical of all when the works in question are both questionable in these respects and certainly not negligible – when, on the contrary, they disquietingly command our attention. So it is not surprising that, looking in this direction, we find ourselves once again confronting Wagner, and that the question of Wagner refuses to go away.

It is foolish to try to say anything briefly about this subject. However, the extreme and, in itself, untypical case of Wagner helps to make a point about the interrelation of musicology and the re-creation of music drama, a point that parallels, in a certain way, the point already made about scholarship and purely musical re-creation.

I take three points as given: (1) Wagner's works are worth worrying about; (2) there is much that is ethically and politically disturbing about him; (3) there is some relation between (1) and (2), and merely appealing to a distinction between the man and the work will not, in this case, be enough (which is not to say that there are not other cases in which it would be enough). Much recent Wagner scholarship – or in the case of a lot of the writing about him – has tried to deal with these three points in an inadequate, external, way. Having catalogued Wagner's more appalling attitudes, these writers try to find signs of them in the works, in the representations of Mime, Klingsor, Beckmesser or elsewhere. The present question is not whether these pieces of decipherment are correct. The point is that even if they are, they are too trivial for the writers' own purpose. These are people who accept (1); indeed, for most of them the works of Wagner are overwhelming, marvellous. This is why they have a problem. But if that is true, then the existence of some tiny and disputable anti-Semitic signatures in the works is neither here nor there. These writers have externalised the problem, moving it from where it truly belongs: not accepting (3) at the right level, they are saying that there had *better* be something wrong with the works, and they have come up with a circumscribed and relatively painless way of that being so. They are rather like someone who took Aschenbach's problems, in *Death in Venice*, to be not Tadzio and his own feelings but the cholera.

There is an analogy to this in some of the disputable devices of production. Here, it is not that the comments are very small – on the contrary, the political comments are in many cases very pervasive. The analogy is that in many cases – by no means in all – they are external to the content of the work, and that they are indeed just comments. The *mise-en-scène*, in the worse cases, does not present the work, but acts as an ongoing subjoined ethical health warning.

A long time ago Thomas Mann had seen a lot deeper into all this. His famous lecture 'The Sorrows and Grandeur of Richard Wagner' is still the most helpful reflection that I know in relation to these questions, with the one significant qualification that neither here, nor (yet more remarkably) in pieces written during and after the Second World War, did Mann mention Wagner's anti-Semitism. His discussion is centred on the point I labelled (3) – that if there is something bad or ambivalent or suspect about Wagner, it is there in his work, and it is this that has to be understood. In discussing this fundamental point, Mann mentions many significant matters.

He stresses that Wagner's work shares a German tradition, which has a long history, of the avoidance of or despair about the political. He also points to the fact that Wagner, like Ibsen, had a typically nineteenth-century concern with negotiating relations between psychology and myth, and that he was more successful with this in some places than in others (notably in *Tristan* Act III and in *Parsifal*). It is perhaps worth suggesting – Mann himself does not do so – that Wagner in these respects can be seen as an inverse of Ibsen. In works such as *The Wild Duck* Ibsen was able to give an almost Sophoclean strength and sense of necessity to what is on the outside an expressly bourgeois drama, while Wagner's characters tend to have mythic clothes but a quintessentially nineteenth-century psychology.

Another of Mann's points is that while the old criticism that Wagner's music is not really musical was absurd, nevertheless it was not unintelligible: Wagner's work does break down lines between the musical and the literary. As Mann, in a highly typical sentence, says about the E flat chord that starts *Rheingold*, 'It was an acoustic concept: the concept of the beginning of all things. Music has been here pressed into service in an imperiously dilettante fashion in order to represent a mythical concept.'

Musicology is in a position to take such thoughts further, and indeed in much distinguished work on Wagner it has done so. I point to this set of questions for two reasons. First, it is an illustration of the power of musicology. The business of tracing the connections between all these thoughts – the history, the intellectual background, the traditions, and the style that Wagner evolved – calls on musicology in very many of its aspects; it demands a unity of cultural and musical understanding that makes the most rigorous demands on the subject. Second, such studies must potentially be in the service of production, for if we can understand more deeply and less anecdotally what these works are, we can understand better how to present them in ways that make sense of them to us.

However, part of the real ethical and political problem about Wagner is that we may never be able to reach the kind of position that Sellars achieved with *Theodora*. It may be that the total unity of psychology, myth and ethically redemptive significance to which Wagner aspired is an illusion, not just in the sense that it is unattainable – that is true of Beethoven's ideals of freedom – but because, as Nietzsche said, it rests ultimately on a lie. If so, then no honest production can make it work. We can do it justice – but then it comes out guilty. Or it can come out less guilty – but then production will have negotiated this, as an accommodation between what Wagner believed and hoped to express, and what we can, now, decently and, as we say, in all honesty, accept.

I do not know whether this will ultimately prove to be so. But I suggest that it is a musicological problem in the broadest sense, and so illustrates how many things a musicological problem can be: one that calls on musical analysis, musical history, cultural history, political philosophy; and which, finally, demands an ethical clear-sightedness in recognising what we can honestly accept as saying something serious, which means – as of course it means – saying something serious to us now.

16

Naïve and Sentimental Opera Lovers

This essay was written for a volume by his friends celebrating Isaiah Berlin

Isaiah Berlin used to maintain, particularly in his article 'The "Naïveté" of Verdi',[1] that Verdi was the last great artist who was, in Schiller's terms, 'naïve' rather than 'sentimental'. He went on to mention, as he does in the article, formidable lists of artists who fall on one side or another of the distinction, Verdi finding himself with Homer, Shakespeare, Bach, Rubens, Pushkin and Dickens, while the *sentimentalisch,* in Schiller's sense of the term, include, among many others, Euripides, Virgil, Ariosto, Dostoevsky, Flaubert and Wagner.

The distinction is one of self-consciousness. 'The poet is either himself nature: or he seeks her,' Schiller said, and the idea is that the 'naïve' artist can take for granted certain unities – of thought and feeling, of man and nature – that the 'sentimental' has to seek as an ideal. Verdi, though a late example of the 'naïve', was for Isaiah Berlin a paradigm of it in all its aspects: 'perhaps the last complete, self-fulfilled creator, absorbed in his art; at one with it; seeking to use it for no ulterior purpose, the god wholly concealed by his works ... wholly, even grimly, impersonal, drily objective, at one with his music'. By contrast, the 'sentimental' spirit tries to make art a vehicle for something beyond itself, so that the political outlook of the artist, for instance, may become essential material for appreciating the work, as it is not in Verdi's case, despite the involvement of his life with politics. Verdi does not want opera to be or do anything but what opera is and does; he lacks what Isaiah calls the 'self-conscious, extra-musical, "sentimental" faith in music as a messianic rebirth of the spirit'.[2]

As with all distinctions, there are other discriminations that this one does not help one to make. Intense artistic self-consciousness and a sense of belatedness need not carry with them extra-artistic aspirations: the very idea of art for art's sake, indeed, expresses the one in rejecting the other. There are composers of opera who are paradigmatically 'sentimental' by all the other tests, but whose self-consciousness is precisely engaged with the art itself, to the exclusion of those other aspirations: Berg is surely one, and Debussy another. But it does not matter that the ideas deployed in the distinction can be taken apart and arranged in different ways. What matters is how it is applied to Verdi, and in this, as in any other interesting application of it, the terms of the distinction are not formed simply by some abstract and general idea of the 'sentimental'. Although he is not specifically picked out as doing so, there is surely a particular artist who embodies the half of the contrast, as Isaiah has expressed it, and represents Verdi's spiritual and artistic opposite. Every mark of the 'sentimental' in Isaiah's characterisation of it might have been expressly formulated to apply to Wagner, from obsessional self-consciousness and the need to reinvent the means of expression, to the urge to issue manifestos and to achieve redemption through art; and the malaise of the nineteenth century from which, as Isaiah says, Verdi was remote was the condition of much of Wagner's work.

The contrast between Verdi and Wagner is extreme, over-determined, and just for that reason it can serve as the occasion of many different discussions – about Italian and German culture, obviously (the contrast that was closest to Verdi's own heart), or about different strains of Romanticism. I should like to use the contrast here as the focus of a more modest set of reflections, about what it is to be an opera lover. I am encouraged to think about the question by Isaiah's love for opera. Someone who has had the good fortune to go to many performances with him and to talk often about opera with him might reasonably think that his love for opera just was love for opera, in its purest and best form, and if you understand how he loved it, then you understand what it is for opera, as such, to command the sort of love it commands. This is, indeed, true. But the problem of Wagner leads (as that problem often does) to an interesting question, of the ways in which opera can command love. As the Marschallin says in one of the most *sentimentalisch*, as well as sentimental, of all operas, the 'how' makes all the difference.

The opera lover loves opera as a form of musical and dramatic art, and, from this, several things follow straight away. One is that the opera lover does not love only opera: in particular, he or she enjoys non-operatic music. People who like opera but not, otherwise, music are exposed to the interpretation that what they really like is going to the opera, a taste that can notoriously coexist with having no interest in operas at all. Again, the opera lover is not simply what is vulgarly called a 'canary fancier', someone who is interested in the talents and achievements of singers, but is as uninterested in what they sing as some of them are themselves. It is certainly possible to combine the two interests, and to take pleasure from collecting in one's experience performances by certain artists, as others collect performances of rare operas.

Opera is one case in which love is almost entirely expressed in enjoyment. What you love, you straightforwardly enjoy; you look forward to a performance, or at least one that promises to be tolerably good, with pleasure. '*Rigoletto* is the most enjoyable of operas,' I have heard Isaiah say. 'Perhaps not the greatest, but the most enjoyable'; and indeed, it is hard to imagine someone who was an opera lover, for whom opera was a special source of pleasure, who would not agree that *Rigoletto* yielded that kind of pleasure in a very concentrated and effective way. There are a few very basic ways of being held and excited by the operatic stage, and Verdi was a master of some of them: *Rigoletto* is unusual because the whole work is an example of those, as *Figaro* is of others. But it is significant that an honest opera lover, asked for examples of what is indisputably compelling as opera, would have to mention some pieces that are suspect in ways that nothing by Verdi or Mozart is: the trio in the last act of *Rosenkavalier*, for instance, or the end of the first act of *Tosca*, which, with its mounting excitement and the superimposition of a dark baritone declamation onto the rhythm of a tolling bell and religious ritual, is a splendid example of something that real opera lovers really love.

The fact that the powers of opera can be exercised, not just marginally but very typically, by distinctly dubious works, raises a question – a rather unnerving question, perhaps – about the character of opera altogether. Puccini, in particular, despite his great and continuing popular success, has always met critical resistance, and this does not rest only on certain limitations of his range or his musical invention, but more basically on the feeling that there is something manipulative or even cynical about his works. The charge seems to me unanswerable. Yet it is still true that some parts of those works are able to hold us just as much as operas that have no such faults – and those parts are not necessarily less manipulative than other parts, but often more so. If opera is a serious business, how can this be? It is hard to think of a parallel to it in non-musical drama. Indisputably, some great works of music are operas, but the true opera lover loves more operas than those. Is it true, perhaps, as some musicians suggest, that the passion of an 'opera lover' is not really an artistic taste at all, that it has something undiscriminating about it, that it is not too choosy about where it finds its pleasures? I was once (embarrassingly) introduced to Dietrich Fischer-Dieskau as 'a great lover of opera'. 'Ah,' the distinguished artist replied, 'I am not.'

I think that there is an explanation of why opera is peculiar in this way. (It will not satisfy the most intransigently puritanical, but then it is hard for them to be opera lovers.) W. H. Auden's remark that, in a sense, there can be no tragic opera, because singing itself too evidently seems a free and enjoyable activity, reminds us of something very important, that the enjoyment of opera, particularly Italian opera, is inextricably bound in with the enjoyment of a technique. It is not only song, and the fact that it is song, that generates excitement, but the singer. At a fine operatic performance, we are conscious of the singers' achievement and of the presence of physical style and vitality; a feeling of performance and of the performers' artistry is more constantly at the front of the mind than with other dramatic arts. It is because of this that outbreaks of applause (if not, these days, the granting of encores) may be appropriate, as they scarcely could be with a play, even one in verse. Yet opera is drama, and the sense of performance, as of musical intensity, reinforces the drama itself. In these respects, there are contrasts not only with non-musical drama, but, in the other direction, with the ballet, where the sense of performance and technique is indeed paramount, but which, in our culture at least, is less committed to being a dramatic art, and has closer relations with both the decorative and the athletic.

Opera, particularly in the Italian style, presents one immediately with musical artistry, and so, more generally, with an obvious artifice – conventions of musical and dramatic form that are not simply transparent, as blank verse may sometimes be, but constantly manifest. It is just because the pleasures of opera are bound up in this way with an artifice of which one remains conscious that Puccini, though a notoriously opportunistic artist, can offer compelling examples of its powers. In the second act of *Tosca*, for instance, Scarpia's arrangement of his treachery gives pleasure through its theatricality, which is displayed in a way that could not be accepted without the music. It is not just a device that puts us into complicity with Scarpia against Tosca. It puts us into complicity with that device itself, with a certain tradition of theatrical effect, and what we enjoy is seeing the wheels of artifice turn.

The acknowledged display of artifice, Puccini's most characteristic device, affects the experience of seeing one of his works with which one is familiar. Puccini carries further than any other opera composer the idea of securing an effect through the audience's consciousness that that is what he is doing. In doing this, he is exploiting something that is inherent, to some extent, in opera and in the performance of opera, and that is why one can acknowledge the truth of his talent to the nature of opera.

You have to be far gone in sentimentality and hence in brutality not to find the torture scenes in *Tosca* and in *Turandot* disagreeable. I have known Isaiah Berlin to express his rejection of these scenes also by classing them with what he calls 'music that operates directly on the nerves', examples of which he finds equally in *Elektra* and *Wozzeck* and (perhaps more surprisingly) *Peter Grimes*.

The balance between the effective and the repulsive in Puccini is so delicate that one can see how someone who cared for opera might, despite his entirely operatic achievements, want nothing more to do with him. To have nothing more to do with Verdi, on the other hand, would be to have no more to do with opera. Wagner's work, however, this always vexed case, raises issues of acceptance or rejection, attachment and hatred, which are of a totally different order. It also happens to be the subject of the most substantial disagreement between Isaiah's taste in opera and my own. I have been for a long time deeply taken with these works: perhaps I am, mildly and certainly controllably, addicted. What I am not is a Wagnerian, in the sense of someone who is impressed by the pretentious ideology of the *Gesamtkunstwerk* (Wagner's 'music dramas' are no more *gesamt* than other operas), or who thinks that if you take Wagner's work seriously you must regard most other opera as trivial. The attitude that isolates the appreciation of Wagner in that way, if it still persists at all, is just a remnant of a cult that Wagner himself encouraged.

What certainly exists is the opposite view, which also isolates Wagner from the rest of opera, not for the Wagnerian reason that it is unworthy of him, but because he is thought to be unacceptable to it. There are, and I am sure there always will be, those who love music and love opera, but find Wagner anything from uninteresting to intolerable – boring, obsessional, assaulting, fraudulent. This rejection is not simply a misunderstanding or a limitation – though it takes no depth-analysis to detect that in its more passionate forms the rejection sometimes draws its passion from a fascination with Wagner's achievement, or fear of it, or, as in Nietzsche's case, both. The most frequent complaint, that Wagner is boring, can itself, in some of its expressions, attract the same suspicion: as the literary critic David Miller has said, 'boredom, as the example of pornography perhaps best illustrates, overtakes not what is intrinsically dull, but what is "interesting" to excess. Far from the simple reflex-response to banality, boredom hysterically converts into yawning affectlessness what would otherwise be outright panic.'[3]

Isaiah's attitude to Wagner, though negative, was not of these kinds. It was notably cool, firmly rooted among the less passionate forms of rejection. He simply did not like these works. Admired, of course – who could not, in some way? Liked, no. At one time I thought that he did not like them just because he saw them as a prime case of music that acts directly on the nerves, but I decided that this was not all there was to it, partly because of his attitude to *Parsifal*. He invited my wife and myself to see a performance of it at Covent Garden. But having it in mind that the music of Amfortas, in particular, operates not just on the nerves but inside them, I did ask Isaiah whether it was not going to be very painful for him. 'No worse than the others,' he replied, and it was obvious, as the evening went by, that he meant it. Again, it was not mainly a matter, for him, of Wagner's anti-Semitism or what is supposed to be the suspect political character of some of the works. Isaiah (quite rightly, in my view) found the main cause for that sort of concern in *Die Meistersinger*, and for the most part left the issue there, being less eager than many critics of Wagner to see Mime, for instance, as a caricature from *Der Stürmer*.

I think that Isaiah's response to Wagner was in some ways like Stravinsky's:[4] not at all the same in the extremity of hostility, and not the same in motivation, but resembling it in a kind of taste that excludes any Wagnerian enthusiasm. Stravinsky's motivations, indeed, and the special colour they give to his hostility, could not be shared by anyone who was not a composer. The function of Stravinsky's views of Wagner, as with most judgments by artists on artists, is not to render justice, whatever that might be, but to clear a space for his own methods and his own work. It can be a positive help in that task that the judgments should be downright eccentric. Stravinsky's famous opinion that *Il trovatore* is a better work than *Falstaff* is barely tenable, but it is at any rate comprehensible. It is a lot weirder to see *Falstaff* as a work that might have been written by Wagner.[5]

Stravinsky openly declares, in fact, his interest as a composer in resisting the Wagnerian impulse, which he equates with an absence of limit, an imminent and implicit disorder:

> As for myself, I experience a sort of terror when, at the moment of setting to work and finding myself before the infinitude of possibilities that present themselves, I have the feeling that everything is permissible to me. If everything is permissible to me, the best and the worst; if nothing offers me any resistance, then any effort is inconceivable, and I cannot use anything as a basis, and consequently every undertaking becomes futile.

This is a problem for a creator, not for a (mere) listener, and no-one who does not share his responsibilities and his opportunities need share the judgment. It is possible to share the spirit of his taste, but that spirit is not captured in the formulae that Stravinsky offers when he is describing his own processes of creation. As a composer, Stravinsky says a lot about his own need for constraints, imposed limitations and obstacles. He expresses that need when he says, 'The more art is controlled, limited, worked over, the more it is free.' Taken out of the context of the autobiography of creation, offered as a canon of taste, the statement is absurd – the most crabbed academic exercise would satisfy the test of freedom. In another sense, the statement is of course true, inevitably true, but then it does not lead to a taste for one style rather than another: *Siegfried* is as controlled, limited, worked over, as *The Rake's Progress*.

There is a taste to be shared, however, and I suspect that Isaiah, to some significant extent, shared it. It is a taste sympathetic to Nietzsche's famous anti-Wagnerian remark about *Carmen*, that he liked the music of Bizet because it does not sweat. The taste despises larger spiritual or intellectual objectives (here the definition of the *sentimentalisch* reappears), so long at least as those are the ambitions of an individual rather than the resources of a tradition. It applauds a certain manifest formality, and a displayed desire to please through craft. It would be wrong, though, to say that it is a classical taste, if that is supposed to set it against the Romantic: in opera, it will find a great deal to admire in Weber, for instance, and in Bellini.

Much of what this taste enjoys in opera is Italian, but in its admiration of a certain unpretentious elegance and gaiety, it naturally welcomes many French works. While Isaiah would not, I believe, go to the remarkable lengths of comparing favourably with the works of Wagner, as Stravinsky did, a 'sparkling group of masterpieces' by Delibes, Chabrier and Messager, it is true that as he climbed the path to his house in Italy, what was coming through the headphones of his Walkman may well have been, if not some rarity of Rossini, then *La Muette de Portici* or *Le Postillon de Longjumeau*.

It would be wrong to think of this as a taste for good taste. Rather, this view of things defines more than one kind of bad taste. One kind is either naïve, like Verdi's, or wilfully assertive, like Mahler's, and both can be entirely creative. The other, however, is the uncontrolled and revealing dissolution of the 'higher' into the banal, and this is variously comical, upsetting or repellent. No-one can sensibly deny that Wagner is liable to this kind of disaster. It happens in the truly dreadful march and chorus of the knights in *Parsifal*; and James Joyce had a point, I am afraid, when he remarked of Siegmund's much-admired love song in the first act of *Die Walküre*, 'Winterstürme wichen dem Wonnemond' ('Winter storms give way to the moon of joy'), 'Can you imagine this old German hero offering his girl a box of chocolates?'[6]

There can be no such disasters in Verdi, because his style is always in touch with popular forms, and even with *Aida*, a comparatively late work which uses many sophisticated devices, it is simply not a relevant complaint that the triumphal march could be a large-scale offering by the Busseto town band. It is inherent to Wagner's enterprise, on the other hand, that he should run these risks. For the same reason, he can elicit, at his most effective, a more extreme response. The sense of the limitless, which Stravinsky mentioned in describing his relations as a composer to Wagner's work, is certainly involved in the emotional reactions that it can produce. Feelings of being drowned, ecstatic or immeasurably elated have been mentioned by Wagner's audiences from the earliest performances on: above all, of course, in the case of *Tristan*. There are probably not many people now who would want to find in these experiences the religious or revelatory significance that was once claimed for them by Wagnerians, whose rhetoric of transfiguration has done almost as much to put off the sceptical as the earlier cult of Bayreuth did (to which the less devotional admirer of Wagner might have applied the remark made by Monsignor Ronald Knox when asked why he never went to Rome, that if you are feeling queasy on a ship, the worst place to go is the engine room).

Whatever is to be made of them, the peculiar effects of Wagner's music, when it works at full power, are undeniable: everyone who cares for it will know what I am talking about. I remember in particular some performances of the *Ring* in English at the English National Opera in the 1970s. It did not always work, but on some evenings, when Reginald Goodall's patiently synoptic vision took hold, and Alberto Remedios showed what it is to be that very rare thing, a truly lyrical *Heldentenor*, all the limitations disappeared, the creaking space-age scenery seemed to dissolve into light, and it was as if there were no tomorrow. There was a performance, too, at Covent Garden by Jon Vickers as Tristan, one of several that he gave at that time, which was extraordinary. While still sustaining the heroic tone, he peculiarly conveyed the sense from the beginning that this was a doomed man who partly understood that he was on the way to disaster. When Tristan confronts Isolde for the first time, near the end of Act I, he greets her with the words 'Begehrt, Herrin, was Ihr wünscht' ('Command, my lady, what you desire'); and as Vickers sang 'Herrin,' a descending fifth, his voice took on a hollow tone of acceptance that seemed to prefigure everything, immediately reducing me and others to a virtually uncontrollable state which lasted the rest of the act and most of the evening.

It has often been said that no-one but Wagner, at least among opera composers, can cause such extreme responses. In my own experience, it is certainly true. But then one may ask, ingenuously: why should they? This is one, special, form of artistic power; and like all great artistic capacities, there are other very valuable ones that it excludes. It would be an error, perhaps a symptom of real addiction, to suppose that the satisfaction offered by Wagner is one that transcends any other offered by music, and that all opera aspires to the special kind of power that he achieves. No-one thinks any comparable thing with respect to the other arts. But equally, it is a question why this power, as opposed to those exercised by other composers, should be so distrusted and resented. Indeed, there is an earlier question, of how this power can even figure in the thoughts of those who reject Wagner: if one does not feel it, how does one know what is supposed to be objectionable? For some people, no doubt, the answer is that they do feel it, and that is why they reject it. For others, it may be that they do not feel it, but they do feel, and resentfully, that something extreme is being demanded of them. For most, perhaps, and especially those who are coolly unimpressed, the answer may be that without the kind of involvement that leads, occasionally, to those extreme responses, the works appear to lack interest in a particularly annoying way: they seem not works of music, but only causes, vehicles, a pharmacopoeia of emotion.

If it were true that Wagner's works lacked musical interest, then it would help to explain why they appear so differently to those who are moved by them and those who are not. But it is not true. It has indeed been said that Wagner wrote 'music for the unmusical', and the intention of the comment, I take it, is that he solved the problems of organising these vast works by principles of dramatic and psychological association rather than in terms of musical form. The leitmotif, above all, is thought to be a less than musical device. There are certainly passages that invite the jokes of Stravinsky, Milhaud and others, where the effect of the motives is indeed like that of a skilfully assembled slide show. But in general, it cannot be right to oppose dramatic and psychological associations to musical proce-dures in Wagner. His aim was to achieve the associations through the procedures, and it is hard to see how the opening of Act III of *Siegfried*, for instance, charged as it is with the drama, could be thought to fail as a musical achievement, or not to make musical sense.

If the objection is that the musical procedures are dramatically moti-vated, then this just comes to saying that this is not pure music: indeed, it is opera. In just this way, in his integration of dramatic and psychological processes with musical procedures, Wagner's achievements are essentially operatic, and that is one reason why those who appreciate him see their appreciation as continuous with their reactions to other opera they admire. Equally, a lot of what excites them is what excites them in other operas – such basic operatic materials as silence or crescendo, or a generous melodic gesture.

Yet there is also a way in which Wagner's art is not typically operatic, and is even an antithesis to that of other operatic composers. He himself said, 'my art is the art of transition', and some of his greatest strengths lie in the capacity, not only to move easily between motives or keys, but to get from one texture or mood or dramatic context to another. A fine example of it is the invention with which, in Act II of *Die Walküre*, he negotiates a particularly difficult change from the testy domestic quarrel, in which Fricka defeats Wotan, to the following scene in which Wotan lays his world-historical concerns before Brünnhilde: Fricka's victory is marked by a beautiful and unexpected passage ('Deiner ew'gen Gattin heilige Ehre'; 'The sacred honour of your eternal wife') which in a few bars rounds off the first scene and sets the tone for the next.

It is essential to this skill that it conceals itself, that you are conscious of the result rather than of the procedure. Rather similarly, at another level, though great artistry is needed to sing Wagnerian opera well (or, indeed, at all), that artistry is not typically on display – it is deployed in producing, within the conventions of the style, a dramatic voice, which conveys a response or reveals a state of mind. One is conscious, indeed, of physical presence and power (this is a basic excitement that is shared by the experience of Wagnerian operas and others), but vocal artistry as such is less to the fore. The only work of Wagner's in which vocal skill and musical ingenuity repeatedly draw attention to themselves is *Die Meistersinger*, and that is for the special reason that the relation of skill to expression is the subject of the opera – to that extent it is about itself. Wagner is thus the opposite of Puccini, as I earlier described him. The performer's skills, and the composer's, do not stand at the front of the audience's consciousness, and it is not through manifest artifice that he achieves his effects. Yet manifest artifice of that kind is indeed typical of opera, and just as Puccini's exploitation of it brings his melodramas close to the heartland of opera, so Wagner's refusal of it sets his masterpieces apart from that heartland.

It must be in terms of some such account, I think, of the similarities and the equally notable differences between the experience of Wagner's operas and that of others, that we should explain the striking asymmetry of taste among people who otherwise share an attachment to opera: those who appreciate both Wagner and other styles of opera find a lot in common between them, while other people find it hard to see how an enthusiasm for opera extends to Wagner at all. Certainly, there is something to explain, and most of the existing explanations, such as they are, are too contemptuous of one party or the other: the disagreement is not one that invites contempt.

But if these, or something like them, are the differences, where are we left with the distinction between the 'naïve' and the 'sentimental'? There was never any suggestion that the 'naïve' excluded the conventional – on the contrary. In the article from which I started, Isaiah reported the fact that certain progressive Russian composers of the time resented Verdi's work, just because he had succeeded in bringing new life to the dreaded 'formula', the stale conventions of the Italian tradition. There is no puzzle in the 'naïve' artist using very conventional means, and the 'sentimental'

artist using less conventional means. But what about the operatic audience? They are by the nature of opera conscious of those conventional
means, and enjoy them as such. The nature of that consciousness,
however, changes over time. Verdi's means are not available now to a
popular composer, or to any other, and even if his characters are represented as embodying universal human passions, the conventions of that
representation appear to us, now, not just as conventions, but as those
particular conventions; just as we also have to allow for some nineteenth-
century sentiments about fathers, virgins, respectable sisters and so forth.
We may easily accept the conventions, but our sense of them, and our
enjoyment, cannot avoid the further turn of historical self-consciousness
that all this implies. We can enjoy the 'naïve' artist, but only as 'sentimental'
listeners.

With Wagner, on the other hand, though some of his concerns belong
clearly to the nineteenth century, much of his complexity, perversity and
ambiguity is familiar in our world, as is the idea of works as extreme as his.
His musical style, because it did so much to form not just the art music of
the twentieth century, but (for instance) film music, is close in some ways to
what is familiar outside the opera house. Because of their difficulty, their
history and the huge problems of mounting them, his works are only now
really meeting the audiences he himself wanted for them: through such
productions as those at English National Opera, and, on an immeasurably
greater scale, through TV broadcasts of Chéreau's *Ring*, for instance, they
are seen by people who are neither devotees nor experienced opera-goers,
and who approach them, not of course without preconceptions, but
without the preconceptions of those who love other operas and their arti-
fices. To many people now, despite and because of his oblique devices,
Wagner may seem to speak more directly than other opera does. It is the
'sentimental' artist who has the 'naïve' public.

Notes

1. 'The "Naïveté" of Verdi', *Hudson Review*, 21 (1968), pp. 138–47; reprinted from *Atti del
   I Congresso internazionale di studi verdiani*, 1966 (Parma, 1969); reprinted in *About the
   House*, 3:1 (March 1969), pp. 8–13.
2. *Hudson Review*, pp. 140–1, 143.
3. D. A. Miller, *The Novel and the Police* (Berkeley and London, 1988), p. 145. He is actually
   discussing a markedly different case: Trollope.

4. As expressed in *Poetics of Music* (the Charles Eliot Norton Lectures 1939–40), trans. Arthur Knodell and Ingolf Dahl (Cambridge, Mass., 1970). I have no reason to think that Isaiah's views were actually influenced by Stravinsky: it is only a matter of resemblances.

5. *Poetics of Music*, p. 61; the quotation in the next paragraph comes from p. 63.

6. Ellmann, *James Joyce*, revised edn (Oxford, 1983), p. 460.

Acknowledgments

'The Nature of Opera', in *The New Grove Dictionary of Opera*, ed. Stanley Sadie, 4 vols (London, 1992)

'Mozart's Comedies and the Sense of an Ending', *Musical Times*, July 1981

'Mozart's Figaro: A Question of Class?' BBC talk (July 1974), published in *The Listener*, August 1974

'Don Giovanni as an Idea', in *W. A. Mozart: 'Don Giovanni'* (Cambridge Opera Handbooks), ed. Julian Rushton (Cambridge, 1988)

'Passion and Cynicism: Remarks on *Così fan tutte*', *Musical Times*, April 1973

'Rather Red than Black: Verdi, *Don Carlos* and the Passion for Freedom', unpublished lecture

'*Tristan* and Time', in the programme for a production of *Tristan and Isolde* at the Royal Opera House, Covent Garden, 1981

'The Elusiveness of Pessimism: Responding to the *Ring*', in the programme for a production of the *Ring* at the Royal Opera House, Covent Garden, 1991

'Wagner and the Transcendence of Politics', published as 'Wagner and Politics', *New York Review of Books*, November 2000

'L'Envers des destinées: *Pelléas et Mélisande*', *New Universities Quarterly*, 1975

'Manifest Artifice: The Ingenuity of Puccini', in *Tosca* (English National Opera/Royal Opera House Opera Handbook, 16) (London and New York, 1982)

'Comments on *Opera and Ideas: From Mozart to Strauss* by Paul Robinson', republished in Paul Robinson, *Opera, Sex and Other Vital Matters* (Chicago, 2002)

'The Marriage and the Flute', in the programme for a production of *The Midsummer Marriage* at the Royal Opera House, Covent Garden, 1996, reprinted in the programme for the new production in 2005

'Janáček's Modernism', in *Sing, Ariel: Essays and Thoughts for Alexander Goehr's Seventieth Birthday*, ed. Alison Latham (London, 2003)

'Authenticity and Re-creation: Musicology, Performance and Production', an edited version of 'Scholarship, Authenticity, History', in *Musicology and Sister Disciplines: Past, Present, Future*, Proceedings of the 16th Congress of the International Musicological Society, London, 1997, ed. David Greer (Oxford, 2000)

'Naïve and Sentimental Opera Lovers', in *Isaiah Berlin: A Celebration*, ed. Edna and Avishai Margalit (London, 1991)

Index of Names and Works